THE TIBETAN BOOK OF SUCCESS

THE TIBETAN BOOK OF SUCCESS

A Guide to Relationships, Leadership, Communication, and Happiness

Advice from Jamgon Mipham Rinpoche, Patrul Rinpoche, Sakya Pandita, and an anonymous scroll from the Dunhuang Caves

TRANSLATED AND INTRODUCED BY

Orgyen Chowang

SHAMBHALA

Shambhala Publications, Inc.
2129 13th Street
Boulder, Colorado 80302
www.shambhala.com

Cover art: Courtesy of Robert Beer
Cover design: Victor Mingovits
Interior design: Kate Huber-Parker

9 8 7 6 5 4 3 2 1

First Edition
Printed in the United States of America

Shambhala Publications makes every effort to
print on acid-free, recycled paper.
Shambhala Publications is distributed worldwide
by Penguin Random House, Inc., and its subsidiaries.

Library of Congress Cataloging-in-Publication Data
Names: Chowang, Orgyen, translator.
Title: The Tibetan book of success: a guide to relationships, leadership, communication, and happiness / translated and introduced by Orgyen Chowang.
Description: Boulder: Shambhala Publications, 2026
Identifiers: LCCN 2025025623 | ISBN 9781645474241 trade paperback
Subjects: LCSH: Buddhism—Essence, genius, nature. | Aphorisms and apothegms. | Rnying-ma-pa (Sect)—Doctrines.
Classification: LCC BQ4036 .T53 2026 | DDC 294.3—dc23/eng/20250912
LC record available at https://lccn.loc.gov/2025025623

The authorized representative in the EU for product safety and compliance is eucomply OÜ, Pärnu mnt 139b-14, 11317 Tallinn, Estonia, hello@eucompliancepartner.com.

CONTENTS

Introduction: A Road Map to *The Tibetan Book of Success* ix

Why Call This Book The Tibetan Book of Success? *xi*

Values for Both Daily Life and Spiritual Progress xvi

Why These Texts Are Relevant Today xviii

The Four Texts xx

Sequencing the Four Texts xxxiii

The Benefits of Adopting and Applying These Teachings xxxv

The Impact of The Way of Living Teachings on My Life lii

How to Apply This Advice in Your Life lv

1. THE WAY OF LIVING: *The Precious Jewel That Attracts Excellence and Abundance, by Jamgon Mipham Rinpoche* 3

Reasons for Failure and Success 6

Rewards for Having Principles and Values 10

The Ten Powers 13

Benefits of the Ten Powers 39

2. QUINTESSENTIAL SPEECH OF WISDOM:
Answering the Questions of Young Loden, by Patrul Rinpoche 45

Three Levels of Communication 53
Dealing with Opponents 61
Relating with Family and Friends 62
Choose Your Friends Wisely 63
Daily Living 64
The Five Most Important Lessons 69
The Root Cause of Your Problems 74
Conclusion 78

3. AN ARRAY OF WISDOM SPEECH
by Sakya Pandita 81

Self-Awareness 85
Criticism and Praise 86
Communication 88
Dealing with People 90
Being a Wise Leader 92
Being Mindful 94
Healthy Relationships 94
Wealth and Success 95
Social Intelligence 98

Six Qualities That Are Critical for Men 100
Six Qualities That Are Critical for Women 100
Meetings 101
Six Qualities That Are Critical for Leaders 103
Conclusion 104

4. ADVICE FOR A SUCCESSFUL AND HAPPY LIFE:
A Conversation Between Brothers, from an Anonymous Scroll Discovered in the Dunhuang Caves 107

Happiness 111
Honesty and Fairness 112
Receiving Gifts 115
Wisdom 116
Decency and Respect 117
Working Together 119
Giving Advice 123
Leadership and Community 123
The Law 126
Friendship 127
Education and Knowledge 130
Wealth, Legacy, and Contentment 132

Acknowledgments 137
About the Translator 139

This book is dedicated and offered to my enlightened master, Jigme Phuntsok Rinpoche, who gave me the most excellent guidance for my life, and who gave me the strength and confidence to navigate the world.

INTRODUCTION

A Road Map to The Tibetan Book of Success

The Tibetan Book of Success is the first collection of English translations of four extraordinary classical texts from Tibetan literature in the genre of teachings known as "The Way of Living" (in Tibetan, *Luk kyi tencho*). These texts contain secular wisdom that has been passed down through the centuries, with their origins tracing back to the Buddha's teachings in India around the fifth century B.C.E. While the Buddha is usually associated with spiritual teachings on enlightenment, he also offered profound and practical guidance on how to live a flourishing and harmonious life in the everyday world. He addressed topics such as how to govern effectively, how to build healthy relationships, how to communicate skillfully, and how to create a life of happiness and success. These teachings were preserved in many of the Buddha's discourses, or sutras.

In the second century C.E., the great Indian scholar Nagarjuna expanded on these ideas in his writings, such as *The Wisdom Tree* and *One Hundred Wisdoms*. Nagarjuna's works provide detailed advice on personal growth, transformation, and living wisely. Each verse of *One Hundred Wisdoms*, for example, offers a concise piece of guidance on how to live a rewarding life. By the eighth or ninth century, these teachings were translated from Sanskrit into Tibetan, where they became a part of the Tibetan tradition. Over time, they were further developed by great Tibetan masters such as Sakya Pandita (1182–1251), Patrul Rinpoche (1808–1887), and Jamgon Mipham Rinpoche (1846–1912), and many other masters who adapted these teachings to address the challenges of their times—which are very much like the challenges of our own.

At their core, The Way of Living teachings are about cultivating wisdom, integrity, and other essential qualities that lead to happiness, success, and connection. They express universal principles for living a meaningful and successful life. They show us that there is a clear path to these outcomes—a path that is not random or arbitrary but grounded in timeless values.

WHY CALL THIS BOOK *THE TIBETAN BOOK OF SUCCESS*?

I chose *The Tibetan Book of Success* as the title for this book to reflect the origins of these teachings, as they were composed by four great Tibetan masters. When I was translating these texts, people asked how this book would be different from modern-day self-help books. The difference is that this advice comes from timeless ancient wisdom, while still being practical and contemporary. The values described here are not just Tibetan values—they are universal. Integrity, for example, is not just a Tibetan value; everyone needs integrity. Wisdom is not just for Tibetans. Fairness doesn't belong only to Tibet; it belongs to humanity. These principles transcend culture and religion, offering guidance that is relevant to all people, everywhere.

Patrul Rinpoche explains that these teachings come from the wisdom gathered by many generations of wise people—parents, leaders, enlightened masters, kings, and scholars—who observed what works and what does not work in life. Over thousands of years, through trial and error, they distilled this wisdom into clear and practical principles. These teachings are the result of human experimentation and experience, tested and refined to uncover the causes of happiness, success, and effective communication. For this reason, each of these texts is a collection of distilled wisdom, like the nectar of human understanding.

As for the term *success*, some people believe success requires relentless ambition and ruthless competition with others to get ahead. This approach, fueled by obsessive desire and the willingness to win at any cost—even if that means stepping on or over others—may look like success, but it is hollow. It involves ego and generates stress, conflict, and negativity.

The success explored in this book is different. It's rooted in principles, not ego. It stems from integrity, mindfulness, wisdom, fairness, and decency. True success isn't harmful or achieved at someone else's expense—it's cooperative, shared, and uplifting.

Whether in business, relationships, or personal happiness, real success grows from inner values. But how do you succeed without excessive ego, competition, or conflict? That's the focus of this book. The lesson is simple: Without principles, even hard work can lead to failure. Without mindfulness, you may achieve a goal, but at what cost?

Mipham Rinpoche expresses this beautifully:

> If a person pushes too much for their own self-interest,
> even if at first they become a leader, eventually
> they fall lower and lower,
> like water cascading down a steep mountainside.
> If you dedicate yourself to helping others,
> even if you begin as a servant, eventually
> you will rise higher and higher,
> like a dragon soaring straight into the sky.

People often think success is simply being well off financially, and while that is one aspect, there are many others. Success does not mean only material achievement. True success touches every area of your life. It means making good decisions, earning the respect of others, enjoying strong relationships, feeling fulfilled, and experiencing genuine satisfaction and happiness. When your life feels meaningful and you have a sense of purpose, all of this is success. *The Tibetan Book of Success* is about how to thrive in all these areas. Mipham Rinpoche and the other authors whose works I've translated here discuss this in depth.

Even if you are materially successful, you may still struggle in other areas—and that affects how successful you truly are. It's like having a house where one part is in excellent shape, but another is falling apart. If your living room and bedroom are beautiful but the kitchen is unusable, you can't live there comfortably. Similarly, if you have lots of money but you don't know how to connect with people or earn their respect, life becomes uncomfortable. You may succeed in one area but fail in others.

That is why success, as discussed in this book, is not defined as just material success. Throughout this book, these texts explain how to gain respect, help others, find fulfillment, and create success across all aspects of life. Then your success isn't partial—it's total.

Becoming successful also includes achieving a genuine sense of satisfaction, fulfillment, and enjoyment without enduring excessive stress. Pressure and stress arise when the different parts of your life—communication, relationships, decision-making, work, and so on—aren't functioning properly. If communication and relationships are tense or difficult, everything feels hopeless. If you struggle in your effort to make the right decisions, you feel paralyzed. If you can't get anything done at work, you feel useless. Beneath all of this, the real cause of stress is weak inner qualities. When those are lacking, everything feels unstable, and pressure builds. In contrast, when you strengthen your inner qualities by developing mindfulness, wisdom, reliability, and other good characteristics, your communication improves, your relationships become more harmonious, you act decisively, and your work flows more smoothly. As a result, stress and pressure naturally dissolve on their own. With these principles, your connections become easier and more genuine. You become more comfortable and optimistic about life.

Success that brings deep fulfillment, long-lasting joy, and benefits many—where you succeed and others rise with you, where you help people along the way and everyone benefits from the results—comes only from wisdom and values. It's not "I win, you lose." It's win-win. Everyone benefits. That's the kind of success that matters in this world. That's the kind of success this book is here to support. As Mipham Rinpoche says,

> The effort to help others
> is a wellspring of abundance for oneself.
> Vast excellence and prosperity
> are born from this and attracted by this.

VALUES FOR BOTH DAILY LIFE AND SPIRITUAL PROGRESS

While the values emphasized in these texts, including decency, integrity, and fairness, are universal values that form the foundation of success in everyday life, The Way of Living teachings also provide a strong basis for progress in any religious, spiritual, yoga, or meditation practice, should you choose to engage in one. Mipham Rinpoche advises anyone wishing to embark on a spiritual or religious path to first establish these foundational values. He says, "Without basic human decency, deeper spiritual values cannot grow."

When these values are missing, even the best intentions can lead to narrow-mindedness, harsh judgment, and intolerance toward others. What may begin as sincere devotion can harden into rigid belief systems, where faith is twisted into fear, hatred, and oppression of anyone who thinks differently. Such extremism arises when these universal human values are neglected.

This is why the teachings in this book are so critical for anyone wishing to walk a spiritual path—because they ensure stability and prevent a descent into fanaticism or prejudice. With these values in place, spiritual practice is genuine and constructive, fostering compassion and understanding rather than division. As Mipham Rinpoche so clearly states,

> The ordinary honorable way of living is having basic
> human decency.
> The extraordinary honorable way of living
> is walking the spiritual path.
> Human decency is the foundation of all spiritual practice.

Although The Way of Living teachings provide the foundation for spiritual practice, the values and principles in this book are secular in nature, and you don't need any religion to practice them. Although there are some minor references to the Buddha and divinity in the texts, whenever you come across words that may carry some religious or spiritual meaning, you can understand them according to your own beliefs, seeing them in whatever way resonates most for you. For instance, *divinity* can mean that when you live with values, not only do other people appreciate that, but so do higher powers; or that if you express positive energy, it naturally attracts positive energy from others.

These texts are not about enlightenment or meditation. The message is not to become a religious person. The goal of these teachings is to offer a foundation that helps you thrive in everyday life. As Jamgon Mipham Rinpoche and Patrul Rinpoche explain, these teachings are meant to support personal growth on a practical level, to transform your day-to-day experience. But if you do wish to go deeper and engage with a spiritual or meditative path, these teachings are indispensable.*

WHY THESE TEXTS ARE RELEVANT TODAY

The teachings in *The Tibetan Book of Success* were written centuries ago but are as relevant today as when they were written because they address universal challenges that transcend time and culture. Loneliness, stress, unhappiness, and disconnection are not new problems, but they have become especially prevalent in our modern world. These texts emphasize that the root of these struggles lies in the loss of universal principles and values—qualities such as wisdom, integrity, fairness, and mindfulness. Without these guiding

* For readers who do wish to go deeper on the path of meditation that these teachings help prepare you for, my book *Our Pristine Mind: A Practical Guide to Unconditional Happiness* (Shambhala Publications, 2016) explores the nature of consciousness, reveals the vast potential of your own mind, and offers guidance on how to experience lasting, unconditional happiness through meditation.

principles, people lose trust in one another, relationships break down, and societies fall into disorder.

The authors of these texts begin by describing the state of the world during their times. They point out how nations were suffering, justice had broken down, and people were disconnected. These challenges are not unique to their eras—they have arisen repeatedly throughout history. When people lose touch with universal principles and values, societies fall into turmoil. Corruption spreads, trust erodes, and people follow foolishness instead of wisdom.

People often ask, "What should I do? My life is so challenging." They feel stuck or hopeless, as if there are no real solutions. But when you begin practicing these principles, confusion and powerlessness fall away. Life becomes smoother, more manageable, and more fulfilling. So for those who feel hesitant or believe it's too difficult to develop these qualities—if you want to live with ease, even just as a simple human being in this complex world, these qualities are essential. Everyone needs them.

THE FOUR TEXTS

Each of the four texts* included in this compilation offers distinct insights into how to live a meaningful, successful, and harmonious life. Together, they form a comprehensive guide to personal growth, effective communication, leadership, and relationships—practical wisdom for navigating life's challenges.

"The Way of Living," by Jamgon Mipham Rinpoche

The first text, "The Way of Living: The Precious Jewel That Attracts Excellence and Abundance," was written by Jamgon Mipham Rinpoche—my favorite author. I truly love and find deep joy in reading his writings and listening to his "*vajra* songs" (songs of meditation experience). Since childhood, I've been profoundly inspired by him. Even after many years, his poems and songs still give me goose bumps.

Mipham Rinpoche was a prolific writer whose wisdom extended across many fields of knowledge. His body of work spans a remarkable range of subjects, including po-

* A note on the translations: Headings that were not part of the original texts have been inserted for ease of reading. Some verses have been rearranged for clarity. A few portions of the original works deemed less central to the main purpose of this book have not been included.

etry, astronomy, medicine, philosophy, and the full spectrum of Buddhist teachings. He is particularly known for his profound and transformative writings on Dzogchen.* Often, I'm left speechless by the sheer beauty of his writings; they bring me such joy and inspiration that words feel inadequate.

Throughout Tibet, renowned lamas admired Mipham Rinpoche as an extraordinary master and frequently invited him to come teach. As a result, he traveled from place to place to provide teachings to their students and communities. He also did retreats in hermitages in mountain sites or caves for three, four, or five years at a time. His life consisted of a combination of traveling, teaching, writing, and doing retreats.

His writings didn't emerge from extensive planning; they flowed spontaneously, like a river. He dated many of his works, providing clear evidence of how quickly he could produce hundreds of pages. He was a rare and remarkable being. Today, his works are studied by poets, doctors, scholars, and meditators alike. In Tibet, his teachings remain foundational—and now, they are beginning to spread across the world.

* Dzogchen ("Great Perfection") is an ancient form of Buddhist practice, considered to be the most direct path to realizing our true nature.

My own teacher, the enlightened Jigme Phuntsok Rinpoche, often spoke of Mipham Rinpoche. On one occasion, he told a story—when a person would approach Mipham Rinpoche to request teachings or become his student, he didn't ask questions about their studies or practice. Instead, he would first ask, "Do you have a good character? What are your qualities? What kind of person are you?" Even if someone claimed to have done extensive practice, Mipham Rinpoche would say, "That doesn't matter to me. First you need to have a good character. Do you have integrity? Are you a decent human being? If so, then we can work together. If you want to follow the dharma and meditate, basic human decency is essential. Without it, I cannot help you. If you develop those qualities, I will accept you as a student."

This story left a deep impression on me. My teacher shared it to remind us of what truly matters. To be a good practitioner—or simply a good human being—one must begin with good character. That's why The Way of Living teachings are so important. Jigme Phuntsok Rinpoche consistently encouraged his students to cultivate inner qualities, just as Mipham Rinpoche taught.

At the core of this text by Mipham Rinpoche are the "ten powers," which he identifies as the key to solving life's problems and difficulties and achieving success and abundance. He explains that people struggle with relationships, communication, leadership, and personal growth because they lack principles and values. The solution, he says, is to cultivate these ten powers. He provides detailed advice on how to cultivate each power and explains the benefits they bring. By cultivating these powers, you can transform your life, resolve chaos, and attract happiness, prosperity, and good fortune—as naturally as a magnet attracts iron.

Mipham Rinpoche defines the ten powers as follows:

1. *Wisdom*: The ability to make good judgments and distinguish between what to accept and what to reject. Wisdom is essential for clarity and direction in life.
2. *Integrity*: Unwavering character marked by stability, reliability, and certainty. Integrity is the foundation of trust and all other qualities.
3. *Decency*: A universal sense of basic goodness that transcends time, place, and culture. Decency earns respect and appreciation from others.
4. *Mindfulness*: Attention to thoughts, feelings, and the surrounding world, paired with an appreciation of reality's fundamental truths. Mindfulness prevents carelessness and ensures thoughtful action.

5. *Fairness*: Treating everyone impartially, without bias or favoritism. Fairness fosters trust and harmony in relationships.
6. *Reliability*: Keeping promises to yourself and others. Reliability strengthens connections and builds credibility.
7. *Gratitude*: Recognizing, acknowledging, and appreciating the positive actions and contributions of others. Gratitude deepens relationships and fosters goodwill.
8. *Helpfulness*: Supporting and assisting others without expecting anything in return. Helpfulness creates a ripple effect of positivity and cooperation.
9. *Faith*: Trust in good qualities, fundamental truths, and the reality of cause and effect. Faith provides resilience and a sense of purpose.
10. *Generosity*: Using wealth, time, and positive attitudes to create a beneficial impact on the world. Generosity enriches both the giver and the receiver.

Mipham Rinpoche explains that these ten powers are interconnected, like the parts of a tree. Wisdom and integrity form the roots, providing stability and nourishment. Decency and mindfulness are the trunk, supporting the structure. Fairness and reliability are the branches, extending outward to create connections. Gratitude and helpfulness are the leaves, adding vibrancy and life. Faith and generosity are the flowers, which ripen into the fruit of happiness and renown. Without the roots of wisdom and integrity, the tree cannot grow. Without the other powers, it cannot flourish.

The text also diagnoses common problems such as failure, miscommunication, and stress, and shows how the ten powers can resolve them. For example, wisdom helps you make better decisions, fairness generates trust, and reliability strengthens relationships. Mipham Rinpoche emphasizes that if you lack these principles and values, your life will feel chaotic and out of control. But if you truly develop the ten powers, your problems will disappear, and happiness and success will naturally come to you.

"Quintessential Speech of Wisdom," by Patrul Rinpoche

The next text, "Quintessential Speech of Wisdom: Answering the Questions of Young Loden," was written by Patrul Rinpoche, a master renowned for his ability to teach profound truths to anyone, from the most educated monks and scholars to the simplest countryfolk. Patrul Rinpoche's life was extraordinary. He didn't confine himself to monasteries, thrones, or caves. Instead, he traveled extensively, staying in ordinary people's homes and living among them in disguise. He worked as a babysitter, a shepherd, and in other humble roles, all while hiding his identity. The moment someone discovered he was an extraordinary master, he would disappear. This unique approach gave him a deep understanding of human nature and relationships, which he distilled into his teachings.

This text is a master class in communication, offering some of the most practical and profound advice on the subject. Patrul Rinpoche organizes all communication into three dynamics based on how we interact with people in different positions relative to us: those in higher positions, our peers, and those in lower positions. He explains that mastering these three dynamics allows us to communicate effectively with everyone, creating win-win relationships and fostering success and happiness.

For people in higher positions such as elders, teachers, mentors, or bosses, Patrul Rinpoche emphasizes the importance of respect and honor. Demonstrating respect builds authentic connections and opens the door to effective communication. Without it, relationships break down and opportunities are lost. Many people, he notes, struggle with this concept, often speaking with entitlement or disrespect, which leads to severed connections, such as being fired or losing trust.

When communicating with peers—friends, acquaintances, siblings, spouses, or colleagues—Patrul Rinpoche highlights the critical role of self-awareness. He warns against always blaming others when problems arise. Instead, he advises reflecting on your own role in the situation, taking responsibility, and apologizing when necessary. Without self-awareness, communication with peers becomes strained and relationships deteriorate. Patrul Rinpoche encourages treating peers with love, understanding, patience, and fairness while remaining mindful of how your actions contribute to the dynamic.

For those in lower positions, such as children, employees, or students, he advises against belittling or dismissing them. Instead, he urges treating them with compassion and kindness. By doing so, you earn their respect and create a positive, effective relationship.

If you master these three dynamics of communication, Patrul Rinpoche explains, you can connect with anyone. Success, happiness, and leadership all stem from the ability to communicate effectively. Those in higher positions will respect and like you, peers will appreciate you, and those in lower positions will admire you. Communication, he asserts, is the foundation of all relationships and achievements.

This text also addresses a common issue: Even when people know the principles of good communication and behavior, they often fail to apply them. Why? Because negative emotions—such as anger, jealousy, or arrogance—control their minds. He stresses the importance of taming these emotions, as they are the primary obstacles to success and happiness. The fewer negative emotions you have, the more successful and content you become through the art of communication and emotional mastery.

"An Array of Wisdom Speech," by Sakya Pandita

The third text, "An Array of Wisdom Speech," was written by Sakya Pandita—a principal founder and revered master of the Sakya tradition, one of the major Buddhist schools of Tibet. He was among the most learned figures of his time, a highly respected authority on a wide range of subjects, including Buddhist philosophy, poetry, and other classical subjects. Fluent in Sanskrit and a master of logic, he won a public debate against a renowned Hindu scholar. He was eventually invited to the court of Koden Khan (grandson of Genghis Khan) and lived and taught in Mongolia for many years. He later taught in regions of Han China and beyond. He passed away in northern China, but his influence endures through his writings and the legacy he left in the Sakya lineage.

Written in a style that feels strikingly contemporary, Sakya Pandita's teachings are often organized into numbered lists, offering clear and concise advice on a wide range of topics. He addresses nearly every aspect of life, from how to choose friends and avoid harmful relationships to how to communicate effectively and lead wisely. The central theme of this text is what we might today call social and emotional intelligence—understanding how your speech and actions affect others and anticipating their reactions. With this understanding, Sakya Pandita explains, you can navigate relationships and situations skillfully, almost as if you can predict your future. You learn that how you speak and act will influence whether people will be happy and appreciate you or feel hurt and withdraw from you.

Sakya Pandita's teachings on communication and social intelligence are practical and detailed. He emphasizes the importance of mindfulness in speech and action, offering a humorous yet sharp observation. He says, "At any moment, countless thoughts, emotions, and reactions can run through your mind. If they don't also run from your mouth, you are truly a wise person." This direct style is characteristic of his writing, making his advice easy to understand and apply. Patrul Rinpoche echoes a similar sentiment in his teachings, saying, "A fool is a person who talks about every thought they have. A pig is an animal who eats any food it sees."

Both Sakya Pandita and Patrul Rinpoche emphasize the importance of thinking before speaking or acting. Wisdom, they explain, is more than following emotions or impulses; individual feelings, while important, are not inherently guided by wisdom. When people act based on unchecked emotions such as anger, sadness, or jealousy, they often create problems for themselves and others. Wisdom, on the other hand, allows you to manage and relate to emotions skillfully, ensuring that your actions and words lead to positive outcomes rather than harm.

Sakya Pandita's insights into communication and social intelligence are deeply practical. He shows how thoughtful speech and mindful actions can prevent unnecessary conflict, foster trust, and bring happiness to yourself and those around you. His lessons are not abstract or philosophical; they are grounded in real-life situations and offer clear guidance for living with awareness and intention.

"Advice for a Successful and Happy Life," from the Dunhuang Caves

The final text, "Advice for a Successful and Happy Life: A Conversation Between Brothers," comes from the Dunhuang cave complex in the Gansu province of northwestern China, now a UNESCO World Heritage site. Dunhuang was an important hub along one of the main routes of the Silk Road, where Tibetans, Han Chinese, and Mongolians would stop and leave their mark. The Dunhuang Caves hold thousands of ancient Tibetan and Chinese artifacts and literary works. In one section called the Library Cave, a great number of eighth- to tenth-century Tibetan scriptures—some of them Dzogchen texts—were discovered. Many of these were taken away by early-twentieth-century explorers and are now in institutions like the British Library and the Bibliothèque nationale de France. When I was in Paris, I was thrilled to hold and read these early Dzogchen manuscripts firsthand. Hundreds of such artifacts remain in Paris and London, and many remain in China. The text from Dunhuang included in this book also comes from the Library Cave.

While the author of this text remains unknown, it is a remarkable example of The Way of Living teachings. It offers wisdom free from religious or philosophical influence and focuses on personal improvement and secular ethics. The first time I read it, I was struck by how beautiful it is and how, although it is very ancient, it feels surprisingly contemporary.

In the text's dialogue between two brothers, the elder offers practical advice to the younger on how to live a successful and happy life. Its beauty lies in its simplicity and universality, making it accessible to readers of all backgrounds. The wisdom shared in this conversation provides profound insights into happiness, fairness, leadership, and relationships, offering guidance that remains relevant today.

Like Patrul Rinpoche's "Answering the Questions of Young Loden," this text is structured as a conversation between an elder and a youth. However, the guidance in both texts applies to anyone at any age. In ancient times, such lessons were taught early so they could be relied upon throughout one's lifetime. Youth is still the best time to begin practicing these principles, but their wisdom can enrich every stage of life.

SEQUENCING THE FOUR TEXTS

Although Mipham Rinpoche's text is the most recent, I have placed it first because once you understand the ten powers he describes, it becomes much easier to understand the values and qualities in the other three texts. Mipham Rinpoche's teachings summarize and organize these qualities clearly, making them accessible and easy to remember. When you've read his text, the values and principles referenced in the teachings of Patrul Rinpoche, Sakya Pandita, and the Dunhuang text will already be familiar. For example, when Sakya Pandita writes, "Sadly, all positive values held in the past are vanishing, and negative behavior is on the rise," having understood Mipham Rinpoche's explanation of the ten powers, you already know what kinds of values and behaviors he's referring to.

Another reason for placing Mipham Rinpoche's text first is that he offers practical guidance on how to cultivate these qualities in your life. For instance, he explains five methods to cultivate wisdom and outlines three levels of integrity. As mentioned earlier, he also introduces the powerful metaphor of a tree, showing how different qualities work together—how some are like the roots, others form the trunk, others branches and leaves, and some are the blossoming flowers that yield fruit. While only Mipham Rinpoche explicitly refers to the "ten powers," the essence of these qualities is present throughout the other texts as well. They are described using different language and presented in different forms, but the underlying principles are the same.

As I've shared these teachings over the years, people have often asked questions like why faith and generosity come at the end of the list, or why they are described as the flowers instead of the roots or trunk. I've found that answering these kinds of questions helps people see how the qualities Mipham Rinpoche discusses—and the same qualities found in the other texts—build on one another and function as part of an integrated whole.

The framework of the ten powers has helped many people better understand how the teachings work together, and I hope it will be helpful for readers of this book as well. It provides a way to see the values running through all four texts not just as abstract ideas but as principles that can be practiced and lived. While Mipham Rinpoche's text gives us a clear, organized structure, the other three texts show how those principles come to life. They focus on action—how to apply these qualities in relationships, in decision-making, and in other aspects of everyday life.

With this foundation in place, the rest of the book becomes much easier to understand. Mipham Rinpoche's text illuminates the essential structure of The Way of Living teachings, while the other texts expand and enrich our understanding of how to embody the teachings. They are like perfect ornaments or accessories to the perfect garment. Collectively, they offer a complete picture of the values and practices of these timeless teachings.

THE BENEFITS OF ADOPTING AND APPLYING THESE TEACHINGS

To illustrate the benefits of these teachings, I'll draw on Mipham Rinpoche's text, which offers the clearest structure. Once you understand the benefits he describes, you'll naturally see how the other texts can enrich your life as well.

Possessing the ten powers is like having ten wise experts working on your behalf. You're not operating alone. These powers support you in achieving your goals. Wisdom helps you make sound decisions. Reliability fosters trust and healthy relationships. Helpfulness, gratitude, decency, and generosity strengthen your communication and connections with others. As Mipham Rinpoche says,

The wise, too, have their own goals,
but they primarily help others.
And in doing so,
they naturally accomplish their own success.

Together, these ten powers act as your best leadership coach, your most skilled relationship expert, your most trusted advisor, and your most reliable guide to happiness.

1. Setting a Strong Foundation

Everything material in this world has a foundation. Houses, trees, mountains, buildings, even the cells of our bodies—everything rests on some kind of support structure that forms its basis, holds it up, and keeps it from collapsing. If the foundation is strong, whatever it supports can maintain its integrity for many years. That is why a strong foundation is essential for anything to last in this world.

But what is the foundation of a fulfilling human life? What allows us to hold together firmly so that our lives have strength, dignity, and an unshakable quality? The foundation of a good life is made up of the qualities we embody and the values we live by. These are what hold our lives together, sustain us, and allow us to live with unshakable strength, confidence, and fearlessness. If our qualities and characteristics are strong, we can live comfortably and at ease. If not, our lives consist of struggle, failure, and discomfort.

The qualities and characteristics that make up the strong foundation of a human life are Mipham Rinpoche's ten powers: wisdom, integrity, decency, mindfulness, fairness, reliability, gratitude, helpfulness, faith, and generosity. If we have these ten powers then our life has a foundation that gives us strength, dignity, and the ability to accomplish what we wish. These qualities affect every area of our life and support us in countless ways. They form the foundation for success in everything we do.

For example, what does it mean to be a good leader? A good leader is someone who embodies all of these qualities to some degree. Every person we consider in some way good or excellent is seen that way because they possess some degree of these ten powers. That is why we speak of them with respect and admiration. All good leaders, teachers, and other extraordinary people throughout history—everyone who has benefited, uplifted, or transformed humanity—have embodied these qualities in some measure.

Every culture describes these values and principles in its own way. But no matter where we are from or what we call them, these qualities are what create the extraordinary. Extraordinary people have extraordinary qualities. It is not based on their name, wealth, power, or fame; those things do not define them as excellent. If a person is not decent, mindful, or reliable, we don't consider them an excellent person, no matter how famous they are, how much power they wield, or how much money they have. The bottom line is that when we say anyone is good, excellent, extraordinary, fantastic, or perfect, we are talking about these qualities whether we are aware of it or not.

In Mipham Rinpoche's text, he says that many people are lost and suffer disappointment, failure, and hardship because they have not developed these qualities. This is why so many struggle and do not find the fulfillment they seek. He explains that by contrast, those who experience happiness and success on many levels—whose wishes come true, who are admired and respected—are that way because they have developed and possess these qualities. The more fully you develop these ten characteristics, the greater your happiness, success, and fulfillment will be.

This is especially important to remember right now. In many parts of the world, we have prosperity and wealth. Our economies generally are much stronger than they were a hundred years ago. Our living conditions have vastly improved. We have made progress in so many areas—we have better technology, airplanes, cars, and medicine than ever before. Yet people's happiness, personal growth, relationships, and mental and emotional well-being have declined. Why? Because people are not paying attention to human values. They are more focused on external conditions than on cultivating these qualities and characteristics. That is why we have so many modern difficulties and problems. For humanity to thrive, to experience happiness and fulfillment, and to connect with others in a genuine way, it is essential that we prioritize developing these fundamental human qualities and characteristics.

2. *Mastering Effective Communication*

In his discussion on the power of reliability, Mipham Rinpoche tells us:

> Whatever you promise,
> if you never break your commitment, this is reliability.
> If you are reliable, you accomplish your goals
> and others can trust your word.

This verse is about communication. Through your words and actions, people come to understand your character. Based on that understanding, they either connect with you or distance themselves.

If you embody the ten powers, you naturally know how to communicate effectively. You instinctively understand how to present yourself. Through strong, authentic communication, you positively influence others. They respect you, trust your word, and listen to what you say. This is the benefit of effective communication. Trust, respect, and the ability to bring your intentions to life—all of these come from communicating well.

Being a good communicator doesn't require constant effort or overthinking. You don't have to keep telling yourself *I want to be a good communicator.* If you have the right qualities within you, good communication happens naturally and effortlessly. Just be who you are. When the ten powers are present in you, success, connection, and happiness become natural extensions of your being.

3. Building Fulfilling Relationships

If you want your relationships to be filled with appreciation, connection, and lasting satisfaction, the most important foundation is to cultivate the ten powers. When you embody these qualities, your relationships—with your family, spouse, partner, friends, coworkers, neighbors, and acquaintances—become strong, meaningful, and fulfilling.

When people are asked, "What are you looking for in a partner?" the answers often revolve around surface-level traits—someone who's "cool," "funny," "attractive," or "popular." But these superficial qualities don't lead to lasting connection. No one truly wants a partner who lacks decency, mindfulness, gratitude, or reliability. You simply can't build a meaningful relationship with someone who doesn't possess those core human virtues.

On the other hand, when someone has the qualities of the ten powers—when they're reliable, grateful, and genuinely helpful—you naturally connect with them. These are the traits people truly seek in a partner, even if they don't always express it that way.

Many modern relationships struggle because they lack substance. People aren't always aware of the qualities they need to develop to build fulfilling connections. For instance, when you're unreliable or lack integrity, others feel vulnerable and uncertain. This lack of depth makes relationships fragile and easily broken. When a relationship isn't grounded in meaningful principles, it becomes superficial and unsatisfying.

But if you cultivate the ten powers within yourself, your relationships become powerful, resilient, and deeply rewarding. People will be drawn to you. They will want to connect with you. They will want to build something lasting with you. They will want to marry you. They will feel safe, protected, and valued. These things will happen naturally, without effort or force, because of who you are.

If you want to enjoy happy, uplifting, and meaningful connections, both you and your partner must possess these qualities. When you look at someone and see that they are wise, decent, mindful, helpful, reliable, and grateful, you naturally feel a deep appreciation for them. You feel connected, secure, and inspired. But when those qualities are missing, something feels off. Even if everything else seems okay, the relationship lacks depth and trust. It becomes uninspiring and unsatisfying. This is not a mystery—it's simply human psychology.

When both people in a relationship possess the ten powers, the bond becomes extraordinary—strong, joyful, and deeply satisfying. That's really all it takes for lasting, fulfilling relationships.

4. Realizing Genuine Faith and Generosity

Mipham Rinpoche says that faith and generosity are like the flowers of a tree. This means the eight other qualities serve as their foundation. This perspective is unique. Typically, we hear that faith is the starting point for any benefits that follow. But here, it's the opposite—faith is the result. When you cultivate wisdom, mindfulness, and the other essential qualities, faith naturally arises. In this view, there is no such thing as blind faith. Mipham Rinpoche defines faith this way:

> Faith means to trust worthy sources of refuge,
> endowed with extraordinary qualities,
> and fundamental truths,
> such as the infallible law of cause and effect.

What are "worthy sources of refuge endowed with extraordinary qualities" and "fundamental truths"? They are identified only after we have developed the foundational values, such as wisdom, mindfulness, integrity, and decency. With those qualities in place, we are able to examine teachings deeply, reflect carefully, and arrive at genuine conviction. At that point, faith becomes steady and clear—rooted in recognition, not blind belief. That is what makes it real.

Generosity is also a flower that blossoms from inner qualities. When you cultivate these qualities, any wealth you possess—whether great or small—becomes meaningful.

You become genuinely generous, and your actions begin to benefit others in a sincere and thoughtful way. Nothing is wasted. Regardless of how much you have, your decisions are guided by mindfulness and the intention to be of benefit. In this way, you use wealth in an extraordinary and purposeful manner. This is true generosity.

5. *Attracting Prosperity and Abundance*

Abundance for Mipham Rinpoche is about more than just material wealth. Abundance includes success, happiness, well-being, admiration, favorable conditions, and all the good things life can offer. When you cultivate the right inner qualities, these external blessings begin to appear naturally.

Everyone values abundance, including financial prosperity. Mipham Rinpoche acknowledges its importance and offers a path to attain it authentically—it begins with developing the ten powers. Here are a few examples of how some of the ten powers create prosperity and success.

- *Wisdom*: The more wisdom you cultivate, the better your decisions become. Wisdom allows you to see things clearly, and this clear direction leads to effective action.

- *Mindfulness*: Having the ability to stay focused, attentive, and present allows you to act intentionally rather than impulsively.
- *Integrity*: When you are honest and principled, people trust you. If people trust you, opportunities open. If they don't, even the most skilled person struggles. Even wealth requires values to sustain. With mindfulness and integrity, prosperity can be managed gracefully and with peace of mind. Without them, wealth becomes unstable—a source of anxiety, conflict, and eventual loss. Think of the many lottery winners who gained millions overnight but lost it all—along with their peace, relationships, and self-respect—within a few years. The problem wasn't winning the lottery, but the absence of wisdom, integrity, and mindfulness to handle it wisely. Without these inner foundations, even good fortune turns fragile and short-lived.
- *Reliability*: Reliability generates confidence. Reliable individuals form strong relationships, make sound agreements, and are enjoyable to work with. Reliability builds reputations and opens doors.

The ten powers qualify you for any role in life: leader, teacher, business owner, team member. If you run a business, these traits help it grow. If you lead others, they help you lead wisely. If you're seeking a job, these are the qualities that make you stand out. As Mipham Rinpoche teaches, these inner strengths naturally attract favorable conditions.

Some people try to succeed through manipulation or deceit. Such tactics may bring temporary gains, but they are never sustainable. In the long run, people place their trust in those with integrity. So how should we respond to dishonesty or manipulation? Both Sakya Pandita and Mipham Rinpoche offer the same advice: Remain principled. If someone acts with malice, don't lower yourself—remain honorable. As Mipham Rinpoche puts it:

> Even if the earth is full of dishonor,
> you should still follow the honorable way of living.
> By making that choice, all good things and favorable
> conditions
> will naturally come to you.

History shows that those who create lasting prosperity share these same inner strengths. Some may have cultivated them more fully than others, but none succeed without them.

Whatever your line of work, if you embody these qualities, success will follow. You may even become the best in your field. As Mipham Rinpoche says:

> As your honorable behavior grows,
> every area of your life improves, like the swelling of
> a summer river.

6. Achieving Happiness and Lasting Renown

Mipham Rinpoche says that when you develop the ten powers, your life starts to bear the fruit of happiness and renown. When you are financially stable, your relationships feel fulfilling instead of conflicted, and you experience a sense of purpose and spiritual clarity, you enjoy a much more complete kind of happiness than the transitory happiness you get from temporary circumstances. Happiness naturally arises from within when you live with these qualities.

As happiness and purpose are based on how you perceive the world, fame and renown are based on how others perceive you. What causes others to see you as good, admirable, or extraordinary depends on the character, capabilities, and conduct you demonstrate by cultivating the ten powers. When you possess even some degree of the ten powers, people will begin to see you in a consistent, positive light. You will be recognized not only for what you do, but for who you are. And because these qualities are genuine, your renown will last. It won't be shallow or temporary.

Many people become well known for their beauty, talent, or winnings. But that kind of fame often fades. Beauty declines. Talents may become less relevant as trends shift. And when the basis of recognition disappears, so does the recognition itself. But inner qualities—such as generosity, wisdom, and integrity—don't fade. If you truly develop and live by them, you remain respected over time. That kind of renown doesn't depend on circumstances. It stays with you.

This is what Mipham Rinpoche refers to as genuine renown. People value you because you're honest, helpful, reliable, and generous. They admire you not because of passing accomplishments, but because of the qualities you consistently embody. And when renown arises from this kind of foundation, it doesn't create problems or become a burden. It supports your life, just as your qualities support your reputation.

If you want to maintain your reputation over time, you must cultivate the inner qualities that give rise to it in the first place. These qualities don't just bring recognition—they protect it. They sustain your name and your presence in the world, without the stress of trying to hold on to something that isn't real. As Mipham Rinpoche beautifully puts it:

> Happiness, well-being, and every form of abundance
> will always rise before you,
> and the great, divine drum of your glory
> will echo throughout the entire world.

7. Finding Meaning and Purpose

Meaning and purpose come from perception. But how does that perception arise? It starts with developing inner qualities. If your mind is filled with good qualities, then whatever you do, whatever you see, and wherever you go, your experiences naturally feel meaningful.

When you possess these qualities, you don't just chase after purpose—you generate it. A meaningful life arises from the inside out. With inner qualities, even going to a coffee shop feels wonderful. But without these qualities, even the most luxurious vacation or greatest achievement will feel hollow.

This is why the title of Mipham Rinpoche's text refers to attracting excellence and abundance. Everything you perceive is a reflection of your mind. When your mind is grounded in good qualities and characteristics, you naturally draw good things into your life. If you're excellent, excellence comes to you. If you're generous, generosity flows back to you. If you don't cultivate good qualities, good things won't come into your life—and even if they do, you won't be able to handle them. When you cultivate the ten powers, you develop the perception that makes your life feel rich with meaning and guided by a deeper purpose.

8. Raising Capable Children and Becoming Better Parents

In ancient times, children grew up surrounded by parents, grandparents, elders, and wise people. Through this close connection, they naturally absorbed communication skills, emotional insight, and life experience. This exposure helped them develop emotional maturity and strong people skills, which in turn protected them from loneliness and disconnection.

Today, however, many young people are largely cut off from older generations. Most of their time is spent with peers who, like them, have limited life experience. As a result, many of them struggle to develop the skills needed for deep connection and self-understanding. Without regular interaction with elders or access to books with ancient wisdom, a person can reach adulthood without meaningful guidance on how to navigate life. If you don't learn these qualities from childhood, it affects you when you're older. Often when we see adults who don't know how to maintain connections or communicate effectively with others, and are still somewhat childish, it is because they never learned these principles when they were young. If you learn these principles as a child, then there are a lot of benefits as you get older. Adults who can function effectively usually had access to good guidance and were surrounded by wise people and a conducive environment for these values to take root. It's a domino effect. If you are exposed to this information as a youth, then it can transform your life. This kind of guidance is useful at any age.

That's why these The Way of Living teachings are so valuable—they offer the timeless wisdom and practical guidance that modern life no longer provides.

When these qualities are introduced in childhood, they become part of who we are, forming the foundation of our character. And with these deeply rooted values, adults find it much easier to navigate challenges, build strong relationships, and achieve meaningful goals. Life flows more naturally when these strengths are already within us. In addition, parents must embody the values they wish to pass on. When parents live with integrity and principles, their example becomes the most powerful teaching tool. In this way, this book also serves as a guide for parenting with clarity, purpose, and heart.

THE IMPACT OF THE WAY OF LIVING TEACHINGS ON MY LIFE

This wisdom has been an indispensable source of guidance throughout my life. I believe that good guidance is perhaps the most valuable resource anyone can have to avoid mistakes, overcome difficulties, and make wise decisions.

I was very young, maybe fourteen or fifteen years old, when I first encountered The Way of Living teachings. At that time, I didn't have much experience receiving real guidance. Of course, my parents raised me well, but they didn't have the tools to guide me in the way these teachings did. My mother didn't read, and while my father could read and guide me to some extent, it wasn't the same as the wisdom I received from these texts. When I went to study with the great enlightened teacher Jigme Phuntsok Rinpoche at the spiritual education and practice center Larung Gar, everything changed. He introduced us to these principles, and it was like being handed a road map for life.

Jigme Phuntsok Rinpoche was an extraordinary teacher of the highest realization. He taught his students about meditation, enlightenment, and how to achieve liberation in one lifetime, but he also used The Way of Living teachings to train his students in how to live a meaningful and successful life.

At first, I didn't fully understand the depth of what I was learning, but as I studied these teachings and began to apply them, they transformed my life. For the first time, I knew how to think clearly, how to make decisions, and how to have meaningful goals and dreams. These teachings gave me a sense of purpose and direction that I had never experienced before. They opened my eyes to the world, and I felt like I finally had the tools to navigate life.

Since then, I have carried these texts with me wherever I go, and I continue to rely on their wisdom for guidance in every aspect of my life. I hold them in the highest regard. They have shaped how I solve problems, how I communicate effectively, and how I help others improve their lives. In fact, much of the advice I give to others—whether it's about solving problems, achieving success, or improving communication—comes directly from these teachings. In my experience, they are among the most valuable principles anyone can learn.

Soon after I arrived in the United States, I found that people were seeking help for living their everyday lives. So, I offered informal guidance and life coaching to many people who came to me for advice. Beginning in 2011, I started offering more formal teachings to groups interested in The Way of Living principles and some of the texts I have translated here. Since then, I have continued to teach and work with people using these principles, and I have seen firsthand how beneficial they are. They ground and transform people's lives. Many students have shared how these teachings helped them improve their careers, cultivate healthier relationships, and develop a profound sense of self-esteem and purpose. Many of these students attribute their success directly to The Way of Living teachings.

The decision to translate these texts was not the result of a sudden impulse. It grew out of years of teaching and witnessing their benefit in people's lives. I have many years of experience working with these teachings, refining how I share them, and seeing the results in people's lives. I have seen how relevant and effective they are in today's world. These are not untested ideas. They are timeless principles validated by generations of masters and proven in my own experience and in the lives of a great number of students over decades. Again and again, we have seen how powerfully they can enrich modern life.

This is why I decided to translate and publish these texts at this time. I believe it is essential to make these transformative teachings available so that more people can benefit from the wisdom of these extraordinary authors.

HOW TO APPLY THIS ADVICE IN YOUR LIFE

How do you apply the teachings of this book in your life? Each line of wisdom in this book stands on its own, like a concise and rich piece of advice. It's like a small, delicious bite of wisdom—something you can savor and be nourished by. You don't need to read and digest hundreds of pages to gain its benefits. Even a single line, when understood and applied, can make a meaningful difference in your life.

The key is to remember what you read. First, take the time to clearly understand the meaning of each line. Then when you act, apply that wisdom to your actions. This is how you bring the teachings to life. It's not enough to read the book once and set it aside. You need to revisit it again and again, slowly committing the lines to memory. This is your training. The more you engage with these four texts, the more they will stay with you and guide you.

How you approach this process depends on what works best for you. You might read a few lines every day, reflecting on their meaning and how they apply to your current situation. Or you might pick up the book, flip to a page at random, and read a verse that resonates with you in that moment. Even if you don't understand everything right away, remembering and applying just a few pieces of wisdom can still have a profound impact.

Many people may feel that cultivating these qualities and characteristics is difficult. They may have doubts, hesitations, or the belief that it's too much to take on. But the truth is, *not* developing them makes life harder. Taking medicine is easier than enduring sickness. Solutions are easier than living with problems. In reality, developing these qualities can be quite simple. The more familiar you become with these principles, the more naturally and effortlessly they will guide you. It becomes easier over time.

Some people already possess these qualities to some extent. If you do, you can always deepen and expand them to experience even greater benefits. Some may believe they have these qualities—but the challenge is, we often forget them in the moments we need them most. Reading about something is not the same as embodying it. If you read this book but don't remember the principles when life presents a challenge, they won't help you. But if you do remember them—and apply them—when it counts, that's where transformation begins.

This book offers tools that can genuinely solve any problem you face. I truly believe that. If you sincerely study and apply what's here, it can improve and even transform your life across many areas. It is like a wish-fulfilling jewel—a source of real change and deep fulfillment. As Mipham Rinpoche says:

> By relying on unmistaken wisdom
> and remaining on the perfect path with integrity,
> you plant the wish-fulfilling tree
> of universal human values.

Most people assume they're "lucky" when good things happen to them—but when you embody these characteristics, you realize that good fortune isn't a mystery. It's a result. It's predictable.

Mipham Rinpoche teaches that it all comes down to cause and effect. When you cultivate the right causes—these essential inner qualities—the effects naturally follow.

He says, "The foolish chase happiness, while the wise create the conditions for happiness." You don't have to wait and hope for luck. When the right causes are in place, good results come automatically.

I don't say this lightly—I truly believe in the power of these teachings. My hope is that everyone who reads this book will benefit from its profound wisdom.

—Orgyen Chowang Rinpoche

THE TIBETAN BOOK OF SUCCESS

1

THE WAY OF LIVING

The Precious Jewel That Attracts Excellence and Abundance

BY JAMGON MIPHAM RINPOCHE

Late Nineteenth Century C.E.

Manjushri[*] is the treasure of all enlightened beings' wisdom.
By remembering Manjushri, you open the door
to knowledge of the two honorable ways of living.
May the courage of Manjushri always protect you.

In this world, these two are to be admired:
Excellence and abundance.
If you wish to attract these into your life
like a magnet draws iron,

turn to this profound advice.
Read it carefully,
contemplate its meaning and trust it,
and live by these principles.

* A manifestation of the wisdom of all enlightened beings, whose image usually shows him with a sword in his right hand and a sacred text in his left hand.

REASONS FOR FAILURE AND SUCCESS

In this world, there are two ways of living:
The honorable and the dishonorable.
The honorable way leads to happiness in this life and beyond.
The dishonorable way leads to failure now and in the future.

The ordinary honorable way of living is basic human decency.
The extraordinary honorable way of living
is walking the spiritual path.
Human decency is the foundation of all spiritual practice.

Without basic human decency,
deeper spiritual values cannot grow.
Without roots, there is no tree.
Without wealth, there is no jewel.

No one predetermines
what kind of life you will lead.
The quality of your life—low or high—
is determined by how honorably you choose to live.

Everyone wants happiness.
Except for the most extraordinary sublime beings,

most people strive primarily for their own success.
This is normal behavior for ordinary people.

Yet by the power of past circumstances and decisions,
some people find glorious abundance,
while others experience illness and misfortune.
Alas, look at the happiness and sorrow of the human
experience.

Without food, people feel starved.
Without recognition, they feel insignificant.
Whoever has earned renown,
success and wealth arrive at their doorstep.

Therefore, from adolescence onward,
everyone longs to taste fame.
Sadly, it is a seductress that
always seems to elude them.

Let's describe the many reasons:
Because their previous positive actions, principles, and
attitudes are weak,
their minds are like tea strainers that hold only waste.
They cling to what is wrong, while the positive drains away.

By showing little respect
to parents, teachers, and elders,
they disappoint the sublime beings who could protect them
and become just like friendless corpses.

Because they don't care about the consequences of their
actions
or the connection between this life and the next,
and they are willing to promise or say anything,
they disappoint those who bear witness to their behavior.

They respond in reverse to help and harm.
If they have power, they oppress those who protect them.
If they lack power, they bow to their enemies.
Therefore, they upset the sublime forces of dignity and strength.

They have little respect for or trust in the Three Jewels.*
What they do publicly and privately contradict one another.
And what they do from one moment to the next is
inconsistent.
Thus, they sadden the sublime protectors.

* The Three Jewels are the Buddha, the Buddha's teachings, and the followers of those teachings. This can be understood as any representation of something positive or extraordinary.

They are unscrupulous,
doing dishonest deeds and accepting tainted money,
not caring if they are seen as deceitful or manipulative.
As a result, they lose the sublime energy within and around them.

By senselessly envying and resenting
the wealth and prosperity of others,
and adopting behaviors that most people avoid,
they exhaust the power their protectors have to shield them.

All the bad choices described here
can destroy everything good in people's lives and
leave them wallowing in a cesspool of their own making.
Even if they call out to a hundred gods and a thousand
spirits, none will come near.

Then they lament, "Why is this happening in my life?
I recited so many prayers; I performed countless ceremonies.
All that effort, all that work,
and none of it helped."

People living in these degenerate times have weak principles
and values.
They're incapable of doing even the simplest things.

That's why they always fail.
You should avoid such weakness.

Most people want to bring
positive and excellent circumstances into their lives,
but like sowing seeds in depleted soil,
they don't know how to cultivate success.

REWARDS FOR HAVING PRINCIPLES AND VALUES

Those with wisdom, inner virtue, and strong values
naturally possess good qualities.
If you embody these qualities and positive traits,
sublime beings will be drawn to you—without ever being called.

If a person is genuine and straightforward,
and always keeps their promises,
such behavior is naturally appealing to the eye.
So, of course, sublime eyes are pleased as well.

If a person repays others' kindness
and has the correct view of right and wrong,

not only will other people support them but
all positive sublime forces will as well.

If a person is resolute and courageous
and doesn't confuse how to treat their friends and foes,
not only will leaders love and appreciate them, but
sublime forces will as well.

Whatever behavior you choose to adopt or reject,
you can keep it secret from other people, but
you can't hide it from any higher power.
Therefore it is crucial to live ethically.

If you keep your word
and courageously and tenaciously pursue a meaningful goal,
even the gods will be intimidated by you.
Of course, other people will be as well.

Your body and mind are the fortress where
victorious sublime energies reside.
So clear out the dust of misbehavior,
and arrange all positive human values within yourself.

Then, without calling,
sublime beings, like swans to a lake,
and powerful protectors, like bees to a flower,
will naturally gather at your side.

If you are protected by divine forces,
even though you are only a single individual,
you will possess the strength of
several thousand.

With divine forces guiding you
as you climb the steps of noble human values,
you will enjoy the palace of
success, happiness, and renown.

You can't catch glorious and excellent circumstances by
chasing them.
This great and steadfast tree
of excellent glory
only grows in the garden of the right principles and values.

People in this age of decline are less fortunate and principled,
and therefore to be broad-minded is rare.
For that reason, even if basic human decency is shown,
it's difficult for most to recognize and adopt it.

People have such little respect
for the best of traditional values and the honorable way
of living.
In the midst of so much dishonor,
it's hard to recognize the right way to live.

Even if the earth is full of dishonor,
you should still follow the honorable way of living.
By making that choice, all good things and favorable
conditions
will naturally come to you.

THE TEN POWERS

The honorable way of living has
roots of wisdom and integrity,
a trunk of decency and mindfulness,
branches of fairness and reliability,
leaves of gratitude and helpfulness,
and flowers of faith and generosity,
which all ripen in the fruit of happiness and renown.
These ten powers are indispensable.

1. Wisdom

What is wisdom?
Wisdom is the ability to accurately distinguish between what to adopt and what to reject.
It is like the ability to see.
Without wisdom, you cannot develop other good qualities.

And how do you identify what to adopt and reject?
By analyzing and investigating thoroughly.
All human failure in this world arises from carelessness
and lack of knowledge.

When people are immature and naive,
before they have stepped beyond their small world,
they do such ridiculous things.
Later, they look back and laugh at how silly they were.

Therefore it is crucial to understand the difference
between what to do and what to avoid.
Having a broader understanding of the world,
and learning politics, history, culture, and more is essential.

Once you experience the highs and lows of life and
have greater exposure to the world,

you find your place in society.
It's very important to gain this broader view.

For all these reasons, those with wisdom
focus on lasting benefit,
consider the long view of the future, and
develop a courageous mind.

The efforts of the small-minded and shortsighted
to achieve any personal or larger goals
are like children building castles in the sand.
The results are insignificant.

Maybe you can figure it out on your own,
but if you don't understand, ask someone with knowledge
or expertise.
Look to their writings and teachings.
Contemplate the difference between what's wise and what's
foolish.

If you follow this advice,
your wisdom will naturally increase.
However much your wisdom grows,
your honorable behavior develops equally.

As your honorable behavior grows,
every area of your life improves, like the swelling of a
summer river.
Each year, each month, each day
you must strive to improve yourself.

You are more invested in yourself than
anyone else in this world will ever be.
If you don't reflect on your own faults and strengths,
how are you any different from an animal?

Even when making minor business decisions,
you must analyze and seek advice.
When making major life choices,
it's foolish not to reflect and ask for guidance.

It's rare to find a perfect person.
But if you recognize your flaws as flaws,
you can correct them because they're circumstantial.
Then you become like a bright, cloudless moon.

Though it's hard to find all qualities perfected in one person,
if you appreciate, cultivate, and

familiarize yourself with all the best principles and
characteristics,
one day you will become extraordinary.

As long as you fail to recognize your faults as faults,
you will repeat them again and again.
While you perpetuate this cycle of mistakes,
your good qualities will diminish.

The more you familiarize yourself with good qualities,
the more you free yourself from faults.
If you remain inattentive and careless,
a hundred years could pass without any progress.

When good qualities increase in your life,
you will become equal to those who were once superior.
You will surpass those who were once your equals.
You will ascend higher and higher.

When your flaws increase without constraint,
like a steep waterfall,
you will crash downward
with no way to reverse course.

For all these reasons, you must focus on personal growth.
You need to overcome your flaws
and expand your good qualities.
You must pay attention and prioritize this.

Gaining wisdom comes from knowing what to embrace and what to avoid.
How do you decide? You must admire extraordinary individuals,
listen to their teachings,
and wholeheartedly apply their advice in your life.

2. Integrity

What does it mean to have integrity?
It means being someone others can trust.
Without integrity, you cannot possess other good qualities.
It's like trying to draw on water—impossible.

Even if all you have is integrity,
that alone is worth more than a hundred other qualities.
Without this fundamental principle,
there's no hope for other values.

You must stand by your values
and never mislead those who trust you.
Such a person is said to have integrity
and is recognized for their excellence.

If you carry yourself with integrity, you are like a lion—
majestic and beyond intimidation.
If you speak with integrity, you are like a sage—
commanding trust and earning the respect of all.

If you think with integrity, it's like having a wish-fulfilling jewel
that grants both your own and others' wishes.
If you carry yourself without integrity,
you are pushed around like a bull with broken horns.

If you speak without integrity,
you are as irritating as a cawing crow.
If you think without integrity,
your pursuits scatter like debris in the wind.

By relying on unmistaken wisdom
and remaining on the perfect path with integrity,
you plant the wish-fulfilling tree
of universal human values.

3. *Decency*

What is decency?
Decency is repulsion to dishonorable behavior and harmful actions.
It is the excellent garment that
safeguards the two honorable ways of living, both worldly and spiritual.

For instance, the embarrassment someone might feel
from standing naked in public
smeared in a thousand kinds of filth
is nothing compared to the shame of indecency.

A person can scrub off grime until they're clean,
and adorn their bare body with clothes.
But indecency cannot be washed off.
Clothing and jewelry cannot beautify it.

Not reciprocating the kindness of others and
not responding appropriately to the negative actions of others
is to be clueless, weak, and uninspired.
This too is a form of indecency.

Ignoring constructive criticism,
turning a deaf ear to helpful advice, and
convincing themselves they can't succeed
is also a form of indecency.

Private information pours out of their mouths.
They disappoint those who trust and rely on them.
When they earn praise and position, they don't know
how to behave.
This too is a form of indecency.

When they encounter the right way of living and
hear good advice, they fail to appreciate it.
They don't put their trust in the wise and sublime.
This too is a form of indecency.

They seek out the worst friends,
wasting their time and being swayed by the misguided.
They turn their backs on the two honorable ways of living.
This too is a form of indecency.

Every day, they drink, gamble, and indulge in aimless pursuits,
destroying what little remains of their reputation.

Every night, their only focus is sex.
This too is a form of indecency.

They squander their time on trivial, meaningless distractions,
engaging in all kinds of negative behavior,
yet feel no embarrassment or shame.
This too is a form of indecency.

They fail to appreciate the examples set by the wise and noble,
and they disregard
profound writings and life-changing advice.
This too is a form of indecency.

To summarize, if you don't carefully investigate
what to adopt and what to reject,
you will stray from basic human decency and the
spiritual path.
This is the foolishness of indecency.

Having decency
keeps you from tumbling into a canyon of mistakes.
But for those who are indecent and shallow,
what's the use of offering profound advice?

Therefore those with decency must
never stray from the path of
the two honorable ways of living.
Always act with mindfulness.

4. Mindfulness

What is mindfulness?
Mindfulness is like standing on the edge of a cliff—
guarding each step with precision,
and tending to every action with exceptional care.

Children are fooled with trivial games.
Adults are fooled with love and hate.
The elderly are fooled by their own failing bodies and minds.
Carelessness fools everyone.

Fooled by desire and ignorance,
people are dragged into the mud of endless cycles.
If their desire and ignorance are extreme,
this path of dishonor lures them to the lowest depths.

Carelessness is a demon's hook
that can snatch someone

from a canopied throne
and instantly drag them down.

Wealth and position are as fleeting as a flash of lightning.
Bodies are as fragile as bubbles.
Diseases, disturbances, and dangers
constantly surround us.

Like a flame in the wind,
nothing is reliable.
So how can you sit at ease,
not considering your future?

The mighty fall.
Wealth declines.
Beauty fades.
How can you not see the unstable nature of the world?

If you don't examine yourself,
and you don't act mindfully,
then you won't recognize your own faults.
Even when others point them out, they will still be difficult to see.

In whatever situations they encounter,
the impressionable are as easily led as dogs.
When others laugh at them,
the immature mistake it for praise.

Just as you measure weight with a scale,
you take the measure of a person
by recognizing the impact they make on the world
through the two honorable ways of living.

For those unmindful and without purpose,
the time from birth to old age
passes like a single day—
leaving behind nothing to show for a lifetime.

Each day the wise practice meditation, cultivate prosperity,
enjoy life, and progress toward spiritual liberation.
By pursuing these four types of abundance,
they will achieve great results.

Meaningless effort and failure
are born from carelessness.
Each day, avoid carelessness
and accomplish something meaningful.

A clever person who doesn't complete their studies
may grasp a little yet act like a know-it-all.
But this is merely a form of self-deception.
This is a fault of carelessness.

Even the broad-minded and wise,
if they procrastinate and delay,
are as useless as a stone resting at the bottom of the sea.
This too is a fault of carelessness.

The actions of the small-minded and inexperienced
are like waves in a turbulent river—
doing nothing but agitating their minds and bodies.
This too is a fault of carelessness.

If a person doesn't have the courage to let go of attachment to
their possessions,
and isn't a carefree yogi,*
yet fails to manage their finances and resources wisely—
this too is a fault of carelessness.

* A carefree yogi is an accomplished meditator whose life is dedicated totally to spiritual practice and who is not concerned or worried about any worldly circumstances.

Not motivated by loving compassion,
if a person allows their enemies to walk all over them
and exposes their own character to everyone,
this too is a fault of carelessness.

Not arising from insight into the illusory nature of reality,
when a person mingles indiscriminately among many crowds
and loses the respect of everyone,
this too is a fault of carelessness.

Not from a freedom from attachment and disillusionment
with the world,
when a person is just inconsiderate, irritable,
and paranoid about themselves and others,
this too is a fault of carelessness.

These and other behaviors
that disregard the wisdom of proper time and place
are the result of the carelessness—
the failure to check and pay attention.

Acting in extremes, without balance,
you cannot fulfill your wishes.

But if you weigh your choices carefully, your progress
becomes unstoppable
like the sun and moon crossing the sky.

How do you know what to do—and what to avoid?
By following the unerring teachings of enlightened beings,
listening to the guidance of qualified, authentic teachers,
and relying on your own flawless judgment.

Advice from any source other than these three,
whether from relatives, friends, or others,
is contaminated by all sorts of concepts, ideas, and beliefs.
What is the point of relying on that?

No matter what you set out to do,
if you proceed in a balanced and thoughtful way,
then it doesn't matter whether the outcome is successful
or not.
You will have no regrets.

This beautiful experience of freedom from regrets
is like a stainless, joyful moon
that rises from the ocean of mindfulness.
Therefore, always be mindful.

5. Fairness

Fairness is the divine path.
Crookedness is the demonic path.
The choice between these two different paths
is the decision to become a god or a demon.

You want happiness and don't want suffering.
Others are the same.
Fair and reasonable people see this and follow the path of happiness.
Unreasonable people don't see this and go the opposite way.

Not appreciating good deeds,
failing to confront wrongdoing,
not recognizing the help of others,
and disregarding great kindness,

when people want to know about your past,
or what you are doing in the present, and
you are deliberately vague and evasive:
These are all signs of being unfair and manipulative.

If a fair and reasonable person becomes your enemy,
that is a product of your past behavior.

But you should not befriend an unreasonable person.
Even if you help them, they do the opposite in return.

When fair people befriend one another, they treat each other well.
Their friendship endures, flowing as steadily as a river.
If a selfish and unfair person befriends anyone,
the friendship may start lovingly, but in the end, they will become enemies.

Even gods are drawn to fair people out of appreciation.
Fair people go to the celestial realms.
The actions of fair people are long-lasting.
Fair people are worthy leaders of nations.

This characteristic of fairness
is the greatest of all qualities.
It is the essence of all universal human values.
What more does one need to say?

6. Reliability

Whatever you promise,
if you never break your commitment, this is reliability.
If you are reliable, you accomplish your goals
and others can trust your word.

If, after careful consideration, you make a commitment,
never break it, even if eons pass.
Be more afraid of breaking your promises
than disobeying the law.

If a person disregards an oath or commitment,
then they are like the leftover tea leaves in a strainer,
devoid of nourishing value.
It is a definite sign that they are lacking good qualities.

From such a person
there is absolutely no doubt that,
like the dwindling shadow of a withering tree,
all excellence and abundance will disappear from their life.

The more you keep your word,
the more others will trust you.

And the more trustworthy you are,
the longer excellence and abundance will stay by your side.

When noble people promise even something trivial,
it is hard to get them to turn back.
If they promise something important or make a commitment,
it's impossible for them to reverse course.

Just as ordinary people value their lives,
noble people value the promises they make.
When the mediocre fail to keep their promises,
the noble find this incredibly shameful.

Noble people would rather give up their lives
than fail to keep a promise.
The mediocre find this shameful
and do not value the special qualities of the reliable.

The mediocre mindset should be avoided;
the noble mindset embraced.
This quality of reliability
is the great ornament of the world.

7. Gratitude

Thinking, "This person helped me in these ways,"
feeling gratitude
and seeking to repay their kindness
is a sign of the honorable way of living.

If you can't recognize who helps or harms you,
the thought of repaying kindness never even arises.
Except for sublime beings,
who could possibly help someone like that?

If you help someone, and they repay you with harm,
they may be human in form, but they act like a demon.
What's the point of engaging with them?
Who would even wish to look upon such a person?

The greatest and noblest people
will generously repay even the smallest kindness.
If you possess this quality,
all other good qualities will flourish.

If a person doesn't repay the kindness of others,
they lack wisdom and integrity,

decency, mindfulness, and fairness.
And without these, what other qualities could they possibly have?

If you recognize and repay the kindness of others,
you are known as possessing dignity and majesty.
This quality of gratitude signifies the presence of other positive qualities.
You are a person who radiates great splendor.

8. *Helpfulness*

The effort to help others
is a wellspring of abundance for oneself.
Vast excellence and prosperity
are born from this and attracted by this.

If a person pushes too much for their own self-interest,
even if at first they become a leader, eventually
they fall lower and lower,
like water cascading down a steep mountainside.

If you dedicate yourself to helping others,
even if you begin as a servant, eventually

you will rise higher and higher,
like a dragon soaring straight into the sky.

Fools are attached to self-interest,
seeking only their own gain.
However, they rarely achieve their goals, and
whatever they do achieve is insignificant.

The wise, too, have their own goals,
but they primarily help others.
And in doing so,
they naturally accomplish their own success.

If you wish to accomplish great things
in this life and the next,
there is no better way than helping others.
This is the path of the bodhisattva.*

* A bodhisattva is someone who is motivated to attain enlightenment, not only for their own benefit but for the benefit of all beings. A bodhisattva wishes to bring all beings to that state and takes diligent actions toward that result.

9. *Faith*

Faith means to trust worthy sources of refuge,
endowed with extraordinary qualities,
and fundamental truths,
such as the infallible law of cause and effect.

Faith is the root of spiritual practice.
Faith amplifies all virtues and inner fortune.
Those with this internal prosperity
naturally behave honorably in every way.

Faith prevents disasters.
Faith is a wish-fulfilling gem
that provides everything one could want.

The Buddha, the teachings, and the noble practitioners
are the ever-infallible sources of refuge.
Always trust and respect
these protectors with immeasurable qualities.

The consequences of positive and negative actions
will inevitably ripen.
Therefore, if you care about yourself,
carefully embrace the positive and avoid the negative.

This life is the field of actions.
The next life is the orchard of its fruit.
Therefore, now that you have the opportunity,
plant seeds of positive attitudes and actions.

Look at people's experience of happiness and sorrow.
The Buddha says their conditions are
caused by positive and negative actions.
Who, then, can afford to ignore the law of cause and effect?

The Buddha, the teachings, the noble practitioners,
and the Four Noble Truths*—finding trust and faith in them
is the greatest discovery of all. Amazing!
It is the result of great fortune and merit.

10. Generosity

No matter how much wealth you have,
eventually you have no choice but to leave it all behind.
Therefore, cultivate generosity
and accomplish greatness in this life and the next.

* The Four Noble Truths, as taught by Buddha Shakyamuni, are (1) suffering; (2) the cause of suffering; (3) the path; and (4) the cessation of suffering.

Even a small gift brings a great result.
No matter how vast your wealth, if it is not used wisely, it brings little benefit.
All the success you enjoy now is the fruit of your past generosity.
If you fail to be generous in this life, you will face poverty in the next.

Possessions come with many drawbacks.
First you gather them, then you guard them, and eventually you lose them.
Even if the entire earth were covered in wealth,
people still wouldn't be satisfied.

Once your basic needs are met,
accumulating more brings no benefit; it leads only to suffering.
But if you are generous, in this life and the next,
all your wealth will flourish like a summer river.

By giving, longevity and honor grow.
By giving, wealth and happiness increase.
Giving is the door to all abundance,
yet people worry about exhausting what they have.

Consider it carefully: If you never give, and only hoard,
you are no different from an animal.
Possessions are fleeting and ultimately have no meaning.
Why not give purpose to your wealth?

History holds countless examples of nations
that squandered their wealth by neither giving nor using it
wisely.
So why not offer even a single bite of food
when it can buy the wealth of a world ruler?*

BENEFITS OF THE TEN POWERS

If you live with wisdom and integrity,
act with decency and mindfulness,
stand firm in fairness and reliability,
and express gratitude and a sincere wish to help others,

if you nurture faith and cultivate generosity,
then both now and in the future,

* In the Buddha's discourses is the renowned story of a poor man who had hardly any possessions. Even so, he offered a few beans, the only food he had, to the Buddha Ksantisarana. For his generosity, he was reborn seven lifetimes as a world ruler.

you will enjoy a long life, good health,
the respect of others, and lasting prosperity.

Everyone will appreciate and praise you.
You will be revered and successful,
victorious in every direction,
and your power, strength, and ability will blaze like fire.

Happiness, well-being, and every form of abundance
will always rise before you,
and the great, divine drum of your glory
will echo throughout the entire world.

So that anyone can attract
all excellence and abundance into their lives,
I wrote this down plainly,
without concern for poetry.

I am well acquainted with the teachings
of the Enlightened Ones, their noble heirs, and the sublime masters.
I have shared them here
as one who knows how to echo their words with care.

From beginningless time, due to deep-rooted habits,
my positive actions have been few.
However, here I have tried to contribute
at least a little something positive.

Therefore, moved by compassion,
I wrote this down for myself and others who
appreciate the honorable way of living.
I also offer it to inspire many to follow this path,
and in response to the request of a wise person seeking
guidance.

Past sublime beings have gathered
a vast treasury of guidance for living well.
Here, I have recorded but a small portion of their wisdom.

By this excellent, positive energy,
may these ten perfect qualities
effortlessly enter the minds of all beings,
and may excellence and abundance enrich their lives.

Gyagar Kunchok, [*] *a being of abundant qualities with a deep love for a pure and honorable way of life and a sincere desire to follow it, requested that I compose a text such as this. Thus, I, known as Jampal Gyepai Rang Dang,* [†] *wrote this at Dzongsar Trashi Lhatser.* [‡] *Best wishes to all!*

* Gyagar Kunchok is believed to be one of Mipham Rinpoche's disciples.

† This is one of several names used by Jamgon Mipham Rinpoche in his writings.

‡ A location near the Dzongsar Monastery in the Kham region of Tibet.

2

QUINTESSENTIAL SPEECH OF WISDOM

Answering the Questions of Young Loden

BY PATRUL RINPOCHE

Mid-Nineteenth Century C.E.

I pay tribute to the sublime teacher* and the Three Jewels.
Please bless the minds of all beings!
Here is worldly advice from an old man's straight talk.

Long ago, in the eastern region of Tibet, in the land of
Gesar Ling,
there was a family with a very intelligent boy.
He possessed gentle decency, a good heart, and many other
good qualities.
His name was Loden.

Sadly, his father died while he was still very young,
so he grew up without good fatherly advice.
He spent his time with bad influences.
He stole and lied and misbehaved.

* The ultimate source of wisdom.

One day, as he was walking down the road,
he saw a white-haired old man with a long beard
moving slowly and shakily with the help of his walking stick.
Young Loden laughed at the sight of him.
"Hello, old man," Loden called out teasingly,
"You don't need to wear that lambskin hat!*
It's not winter yet.

"And why are you holding that stick?
There are no guard dogs here!
You don't need to move so elegantly.
There's no dance competition happening.
Tell me, old man, where are you from?
Where did you set out from this morning,
and where are you going tonight?"

The old man rubbed his eyes, looked at him, and replied,
"Oh, I see. You're trying to dress up in fancy clothes,
but you still look childish and immature.
It's obvious you're trying to seem clever,
but you come across as a little troublemaker.
You know how to insult a white-haired old man,
but it seems like you're fatherless and misguided.

* This is a reference to the old man's white hair.

"Even a solid rock ages.
Even a tiger loses its strength.
Even the same parents can have both a good child and
a bad one.

"When I was young and fit,
I was more handsome than you.
When my faculties were sharp and clear,
I was wiser than you.

"When I lived in my family home,
I was far more capable than you.
I am from the east.
This morning, I came from the land of delusion.
Tonight, I am going to the land of liberation."

Hearing this, the young man thought to himself,
It seems like this well-spoken elder may be wise.

"Hey! Old man," he called, "could you stay and talk with me
a while?"

The old man said, "What do you want to talk about?
I don't know much about spirituality.

And you wouldn't pay attention to an ordinary conversation.
It's better for me to be on my way."

"Please," the young man insisted, "whatever you say, I will listen."

The old man sat down.

"All right, then," he began. "But I must tell you, I don't know much
about spiritual or worldly matters.
Even if I did, in these degenerate times, people follow the ignoble.

"People are selfish, tricky, and cause harm.
The ignoble are more popular than the noble.
The dishonest win more than the honest.
People choose new acquaintances over caring friends.

"Leaders disregard justice,
and the general conduct of the people is a mess.
People reject the positive and accept the negative.
People choose weakness over strength.

"Forget about the next life.
Even in this life,
the indecent and foolish are rewarded.
People no longer value decency and integrity.
Anyone who gives advice is treated badly.
Without advice on authentic living,
no one knows how to conduct themselves.

"In these difficult times,
there's little point in someone like me giving advice to anyone.
But since you ask so persistently, I have no choice but to answer.

"The fox has no choice but to squeal when the demon slaps its face.
A dog has no choice but to bark when a thief suddenly appears.
In the same way, since you ask, I must answer.

"I will speak concisely.
There are two important topics: The spiritual path and the way of human values.

"The spiritual path is taught by masters who rely on the Buddha's teachings.

They teach the *shravaka* path, the bodhisattva path, and the Vajrayana path.*
Their practices include renunciation, *bodhicitta,*† perfect view, and meditation.

"Depending on their capacity and preference,
people practice whatever suits them best.
Ultimately, they cut out the root of all negative emotions
and the cause of suffering to reach complete awakening.

"But the main topic I want to talk about here is the way of human values.
Those who taught this are primarily parents and generations of ancestors,
previous great beings, noble kings, wise ones, and enlightened masters.
Other sources are leaders, officials, and the general public.

"High and low, rich and poor, everyone must learn
how to respect those above you, how to care for those in need, and

* These are three levels or types of Buddhist practice.
† *Bodhicitta* ("mindset of awakening") is the desire to attain enlightenment, not only for one's own benefit but for the benefit of all beings.

how to form close-knit relationships and communities with
your peers.

"The ultimate goal of all of this is for everyone to enjoy
happiness and well-being
now and in the future. Do you understand?"

THREE LEVELS OF COMMUNICATION

1. Respecting Those Above Us

"You must respect your leaders, elders, the wise who
inspire you,
parents, teachers, and everyone worthy of esteem and honor.
You must greet and welcome them.
You must show your humility and sincerity."

2. Caring for Those Below Us

"You must consider how you treat those with fewer privileges
and advantages.
Don't treat them as inferior. Don't speak to them abusively.
Help them however you can.
Engage with them gently and fairly.

"Some people feel important by trying to undermine and
criticize the less fortunate.
There's a saying: 'A dull blade is only sharp when it cuts
your hand.
A useless dog only barks at a beggar.'

"It's easy for people to take out their anger on the disadvantaged.
There's another saying: 'If your ambitions are high, you must
embrace humility.
If you want to win, you must be willing to lose.'

"Sometimes when people gain wealth,
influence, or authority,
they become proud and turn up their noses.
They look down on the poor and less fortunate.
They think they are something special.

"This is a sign that they haven't experienced both the highs
and lows of life.
If you see people facing many different highs and lows or joys
and sorrows,
or you experience happiness and suffering yourself, then
you understand that when you're doing well,
you don't need to be arrogant.

"If others are not doing as well as you, you don't need to
disparage them.
You see that whether you are happy or sad, rich or poor,
high or low,
all these conditions rarely stay the same.
They always shift and change.

"There's a saying: 'It's rare for friends to always stay together.
It's rare for a rich person to always be happy.
It's rare for an expert to never make mistakes.'"

3. *Connecting with Peers*

"Next, consider how you treat your friends, loved ones,
neighbors, and equals.
Without lying, manipulating, gossiping, deceiving,
slandering, or criticizing, try to help them and show them a
good heart.

"Don't get easily excited or offended.
Handle both the good conditions and the bad, and see
the big picture.

"With your friends and in whatever you do, don't be flighty;
be grounded and consistent.

Whoever you befriend, get along with them without pretension.
Put yourself in their place.
Imagine others in your own place. This perspective is very important.

"In general, no matter who you are, be aware of your own weaknesses.
People are often like the pointy end of a sharp stick,
always seeking out others' flaws.
It's rare to see your own flaws as clearly as looking in the mirror.

"If you don't examine yourself,
no friend will tell you.
When you meet face-to-face, they offer a hundred flattering comments.
Behind your back, they spread complaints and criticism.
Even if someone truly caring points out your weaknesses, you refuse to accept it.

"There's a saying: 'If you're guilty, you're so defensive
you jump to outrage as quickly as a horse poked in a saddle
sore.'

"These days, everyone believes they're unique and special.
But true excellence is rare.
Those who study the writings of wise individuals cultivate
personal excellence.
It's very important to be self-aware and to improve your own
character."

Young Loden replied, "You've said to respect
leaders, to treat the disadvantaged kindly, and to relate
mindfully with peers.
These days, you may serve and respect your leaders,
but using the slightest excuse they will destroy your career,
your opportunities, and even your life.

"Similarly, even if you treat the disadvantaged, or even your
friends and family,
very well, they might repay you like an enemy and ruin you.
What do you say to this?"

The old man said, "This is a smart question, but we need to
explore it more closely,
as it's hard to understand without specifics.

"Listen, whatever someone's social standing, be it high or low
or in between,
first, evaluate their positive and negative traits.

"Generally, there are three types of people: Good, average,
and bad.
A good person helps the country and the community,
which naturally improves their own circumstances.
The average person doesn't harm others and accomplishes
their own goals.
A bad person harms others and only thinks about themselves.
Within each type there are higher, medium, and lower levels,
making nine groups in all.

"These days, people offer sky-high praise,
or criticism that grinds you into the dirt.
Such extremes are the problematic behavior of small-minded
people.

There's a saying: 'Don't give praise prematurely to someone
you don't know yet.
Don't run hot and cold with someone you know well.'

"Even good leaders and spiritual teachers have some
weaknesses.
Even beggars and thieves have some strengths.

"It's said that it is rare for a person to have only good qualities
and no flaws.
It's rare for a tree to grow perfectly straight and free from
knots.
It's rare for metal to be sharp, flexible, strong, and dense all at
once.

"These three things are hard to know: A wise person's inner
thoughts,
the deceits of a liar, and the true character behind a smiling
face.
Generally, you need to understand what's in front and what's
behind the facade,
and what strengths and weaknesses exist.

"There's a saying: 'If you know how to analyze, then whatever happens, you learn.
If you know how to observe, then whatever you see becomes clear.'
At first, without careful observation, it's hard to understand others.

"There's another saying: 'Until you meet your enemy,
everyone is self-reliant.
Until it costs you money or time,
everyone is generous and polite.
Until you face a legal complaint or a serious challenge,
everyone is clever and strategic.
Until you go out and confront difficult circumstances,
everyone feels comfortable in their mother's home.'

"Therefore, don't rush to decide who is good or bad,
or who is your ally or your enemy.
You must examine each person thoroughly.

"In general, you need to know that if someone is good to you personally,
that doesn't mean they are good to everyone.

If someone treats you badly, that doesn't mean they mistreat everyone.
Everyone behaves according to their individual interests, their upbringing,
and their interpretation of the circumstances."

DEALING WITH OPPONENTS

"There are five main reasons people become enemies:
because of past karma,
because of your own actions or mistakes,
because others misunderstood you and became your enemy,
because there is no other choice but to become an enemy,
and finally, if someone creates division between you and another person,
and you fail to examine the situation, you may end up as enemies.
These are a few reasons people become enemies.

"The wisest path is to use gentle words and skillfulness
to turn a reasonable enemy into a friend.
If an unreasonable enemy speaks gently but still holds a heart of malice,

the heroic strategy is to tame them with wisdom and deception.
The most foolish path is to charge at the weapon of an enemy you cannot defeat.

"There's a saying: 'If you don't know how to speak, silence is best.
If you don't know what to do, don't try to lead.
If you cannot win, it's wiser to walk away.'"

RELATING WITH FAMILY AND FRIENDS

"With loved ones, if they make mistakes, don't soften your speech or enable them.
Talk directly and help them find a way to improve.
Once they improve, praise and encourage them.

"In particular, don't spoil your children, nieces, and nephews.
Balance gentleness and firmness as you raise them.
Some people don't recognize how good their family and friends are.
They create unnecessary conflict.
Later, when they are separated forever, they regret their actions and miss them."

CHOOSE YOUR FRIENDS WISELY

"In general, the most important thing is to understand people.
One good generation can bring happiness and peace to an entire nation.
One bad person within a generation can create internal conflict and turmoil abroad.

"Normally, if you spend time with good people as friends,
their positive influence is contagious.
If you spend time with bad people as friends,
their negative influence is contagious too.
Therefore, it's very important to choose the right friends.

"There's a saying: 'Positive influences are as rare as gold.
Even an opponent who is a good person can become a friend.
Negative influences are worse than poison.
Even if they are an ally or family, you should avoid them.'

"For these reasons, you should check very carefully who you befriend,
who you avoid, and who you include."

DAILY LIVING

Young Loden asked, "You described how intelligence, action,
and knowing your limitations are important.
How do you conduct yourself and engage in your work
every day?"

The old man answered, "First, your actions include walking,
sitting, working, dealing with conflict, taking care of your
family, and so on.
Second, your conduct includes eating, sleeping, resting,
the way you talk and behave, and so on.
There are good and bad approaches to each of these activities.
You must make your own good judgments and seek advice
from others.

"Learn from your past experiences.
Consider your future.
Adjust to your own abilities and limitations.
Adapt to cultural norms.

"Analyze and make clear judgments about what you can and
cannot do,

what will succeed or fail, and what strengths and weaknesses
you have.
These must be understood thoroughly.
Whatever you do, until the work is done,
bravely and persistently strive to accomplish your goals.

"Don't be fickle.
Don't be easily influenced.
Don't take on more than you can handle.
Be gentle and caring.

"Don't lose your principles.
Don't forget the kindness or cruelty of others,
or who has been helpful or harmful to you.

"Don't be quick to form attachments or to turn away.
Don't blurt out anything that you've only heard secondhand
or that just came to your mind.

"There's a saying: 'A fool is a person who talks about every
thought they have.
A pig is an animal who eats any food it sees.'

"If you act on any impulse, you are reckless.
Be mindful of even small matters.
When it's a critical moment, explain your reasons clearly.

"Whatever you say, speak the truth. Don't overpromise.
Be present and responsible for the people who've taken care of you.

"Don't look down on people when they face hard times.
Don't be arrogant when you enjoy success.
Don't follow people who are reckless or overly emotional.
Don't take every conversation seriously.
Don't take every harm as an enemy.

"Even with a close friend, don't share every innermost thought.
Don't insult people just because you disagree.
Don't have any expectations from someone you haven't helped before.

"Don't trust or rely on strangers.
Don't betray those who trust and rely on you.
Don't feel entitled to the wealth of others.

"Self-reliance is happiness.
Being controlled by others is suffering.
Co-ownership is a source of conflict.
Making too many promises is a source of bondage.

"The best form of wealth is to be content with what you have.
The best quality is kindness.
The best adornment is knowledge.
The best friend is a loyal one.
The best form of happiness is a joyful mind.

"Even an idiot can be wealthy.
Even lions and tigers can be heroes.
Even fish and birds can accomplish their goals.
What's rare in this world is human decency.
Therefore, learn how human decency helps yourself and others.

"How do you distinguish between a good and a bad person?
You must determine whether they act according to the principles of human decency.
You might think a good person is simply someone who helps and praises you,
or that a bad person is someone who dislikes you.

"Don't let your own judgment be swayed by others.
A wise person relies on their own discernment.
A foolish person follows the opinions of others.
If one dog starts to bark, all the other dogs join in.
What's the point of this chorus?

"Whatever you engage in, you need to know your own limitations.
Whatever you do, you must show results.
You need to be sympathetic to your loved ones.
You need to know people's personalities.
You need to know how to use your own resources.

"You need to follow cultural norms.
Your budget depends on your wealth.
The topic of conversation depends on who you are speaking with.
The mind depends on principles and values, and spirituality
is the source of happiness for this life and the next.

"Don't be stingy, but don't be wasteful.
Be warm, gentle, and dependable.
Be fair and honest, and know your limits.
Please don't forget this advice, and put it all into practice!"

THE FIVE MOST IMPORTANT LESSONS

Once again, young Loden said, "You've given so much advice,
I can't possibly remember everything. Can you give me a concise summary?"

The old man replied, "All right, Loden, listen carefully.
Here is the essence of human values, simply and concisely:

"First, be gentle.
Second, know your limits.
Third, have an open mind and high integrity.
Fourth, make good judgments.
Fifth, have a kind heart and be fair to everyone.
All important human values are summarized here."

1. Be Gentle

"First: What does it mean to have a gentle personality?
If you're always angry, abrasive, and cruel, you can't get along with anyone.
Even if you're helpful, people are irritated.
No one wants to see you.
That's why you must be gentle.

"A gentle person is peaceful, kindhearted, and compassionate,
not angry, hateful, or combative when they speak.
Nor are they passive or people-pleasing."

2. Know Your Limits

"Second: What does it mean to know your limits?
If you are involved in too many projects,
it might seem like a good idea temporarily.
But if you don't know how to balance them,
you'll either fail miserably or make mistakes that others will criticize.

"Whatever you do, you need moderation.
Knowing your limits doesn't mean holding yourself back out of hesitation or distrust.
It means knowing yourself, your abilities, the timing, and the people involved.
When you have this context, you know how to engage."

3. Maintain Integrity

"Third: What is integrity?
Everyone wants wealth, romance, and leisure.
But you must think ahead and maintain self-control.

If others get angry and criticize you, don't react, even if you feel upset.

"Remember that actions have consequences, and maintain your dignity.
In the end, everyone will admire and praise you.

"Having integrity is extremely important.
Integrity means that you do not follow whatever comes into your mind,
nor do you blindly follow others.
Your actions and conduct are always stable.
But integrity doesn't mean you have a stiff spine that never bends."

4. Make Good Judgments

"Fourth: What is good judgment?
Whatever you do now and in the future, you must analyze and think:
What are the short- and long-term benefits and consequences?
In this way, whatever you wish will come together naturally.
Without checking or analyzing before you act, your plan will fail.

"For example, there is a story of a king from long ago.
He saw his queens gathered around a bodhisattva and a sage.
He thought these men were seducing the queens, so he killed them.
Later, he found it was not the case and regretted murdering the two men tremendously.
He didn't check on the circumstances, and the result was terrible.

"There's another story from long ago, of a man named Pema Tsalag.
He killed his lover near where a sage was meditating under a tree.
He threw his knife in front of the sage.
Others assumed the sage was the murderer
and punished him severely without any investigation.
Even the innocent can become victims.

"Both of these stories are examples of how when we're influenced by others, or
when others mislead us, there are bad outcomes.

"Therefore, whatever you do, however you conduct yourself,
you must make good judgments by checking the facts carefully and mindfully.

"There's a saying: 'If you don't know the facts, don't say a word.
If you aren't certain, don't swear an oath.'

"Good judgment is
the ability to clearly distinguish what causes failure and success,
what to do and what not to do, what to accept and reject, and so on.
It is not good judgment to focus on others' faults
without any of your own self-awareness."

5. Be Kind and Fair

"The fifth point is that
if you have a benevolent mindset and a sense of fairness toward everyone,
you will achieve your goals and help others.

"In this life, all positive and sublime forces will protect you,
and your wishes will come true.
Others will love you, honor you, and praise you.
It will naturally benefit you now and in the future.

"For that reason, it's very important to have a good heart and a fair mind.

Otherwise, there's this saying: 'If you have a malicious mind,
your actions are self-sabotaging.'

"A good heart has nothing to do
with reciprocity, hierarchy, or relationship.
It is not just for your loved ones, friends, and family.
It's a mindset of good wishes for all.

"If you possess these five characteristics, even if you have no other qualities,
you're an excellent person."

THE ROOT CAUSE OF YOUR PROBLEMS

Young Loden replied, "I see! But even if you know all these principles,
it's hard to apply them in your daily life.
These days, everyone talks about positivity, decency, and values,
but the actions they take are the opposite.
Could you explain why this happens?"

The old man answered,
"Oh Loden, please listen carefully and don't forget what I am about to say!

These days, everyone knows the right values, but they don't
act on those values,
because their negative emotions overpower them.

"Don't allow yourself to be controlled by your desires.
If you do, you'll end up stealing from others.
You'll seduce the wives or husbands of others.
You'll deceive your own sweetheart, and so on.

"If you allow anger or hatred to control you, you'll resent
others.
You'll engage in violence and retaliation.
You'll even harm and abuse your own parents.
You'll start conflicts and legal actions against your friends.
You'll ruin your own reputation.

"If you allow arrogance to control you, you'll denigrate others.
You'll laugh at and look down on them, and so on.

"If you allow envy to control you, you'll bad-mouth your
superiors.
You'll compete with your peers.
You'll criticize and feel resentment toward anyone
who has greater wealth or status than you.

"If you allow stinginess to control you,
you'll be unable to be generous or offer anything.
You won't be able to help anyone in need.

"If you allow ignorance to control you,
you'll be unable to do any good or avoid anything negative.
You won't be able to distinguish what is good or bad
or what is weakness or strength. Everything will be confused.

"The reason for all current and future suffering,
unwanted circumstances, and spiritual or worldly problems
is rooted in unchecked expressions of negative emotions,
ego, and the loss of self-control.

"If you want a happy and fulfilling life, now and in the future,
don't concern yourself with judging others.
You need to transform yourself.
You must focus on self-improvement.
All spiritual and worldly accomplishments depend on this.
Do you understand?

"Listen, Loden!
Wealth has its upside and downside.
Be generous and make meaningful contributions from your wealth.

"A precious human life is hard to find.
Be an ethical and decent person.
Anger and hatred will only cause suffering.

"Wear the armor of patience and tolerance.
Laziness brings nothing to this life or the next.
Have purpose and persistence like a river.
Meaningless distractions are a waste of a precious life.
Spend your time meaningfully and create a positive impact
with your life!

"If you want to help yourself and others,
develop the three types of wisdom that come from
listening, contemplating, and meditating.

"An arrogant person is never pleased.
A jealous person is never happy.
A person consumed by desire is never satisfied.
An angry person never gets along with others.
A stingy person never has enough.
An ignorant person never accomplishes anything.
A delusional mind is never at ease.

"The fewer negative emotions, the fewer problems you have.
The end of negative emotions is the end of all problems.
Since the source of all problems and difficulty
is negative emotions, they must be tamed."

CONCLUSION

Then, young Loden bowed in respect to the wise old man
and said,
"Wow! For a person fortunate enough to hear it,
your speech is like a precious treasure!
The kindness of parents and elders
is like the beating heart of decent people.
Your advice is like ambrosia to my heart.

"I've never heard such extraordinary words before.
Today, the kindness you have shown me
feels like the love of true parents.
From now on, you and I are like father and son.
Please continue to share your guidance with me always.
I can never repay this precious kindness.
I hope to see you again and again."

The old man was delighted, and said,
"Very good, very good, wonderful son!"
Then, in an instant, he disappeared into the sky.

May anyone who reads or hears this conversation between young Loden and the old man be inspired by this advice on living with universal values.
May they enjoy happiness, prosperity, and the fulfillment of their best wishes!

3

AN ARRAY OF WISDOM SPEECH

BY SAKYA PANDITA

Early Thirteenth Century C.E.

I pay tribute to the infinite wisdom of the transcendent,
victorious one.
Through the omniscient one's blessing, I pay respect to all the
sublime ones,
who have the highest knowledge and the greatest wisdom.

I give this helpful advice
so that the reader may
benefit both now
and well into the future.

Sadly,
all positive values held in the past are vanishing,
and negative behavior is on the rise.
Sublime wise ones have passed away.
Idiots are now born.
The fabric that sustains spiritual life is loosened.

Civic and community values are unraveling.
The golden scales of justice lie broken.
The ocean of wisdom once held by leaders has dried up.
The tigerlike bravery of heroic men has lost its stripes.
Respectable women have become shameless.
Instead of following the decency of civil society,
people choose indecency.
Not thinking of long-term outcomes,
people focus on the immediate and trivial.
Rather than contributing to a great society,
they create problems.
Instead of following the wise and intelligent,
they turn to fools and idiots.
They ignore what is excellent,
and look to the ignoble.

But if you follow the sublime wise ones, you will gain the greatest result.
For all who wish to improve their
spiritual or worldly life, I offer these few words.

SELF-AWARENESS

From the beginning, whatever you do,
place your trust in a qualified spiritual master and sublime ones.
If you are grounded in positive actions and good fortune,
if you have the skills and good judgment to set clear goals,
and if you pursue those goals with enthusiasm and persistence,
then whatever you wish to achieve, you can accomplish.

Having a conflict with someone and growing to dislike them
often brings inner turmoil and discouragement.
There are so many areas where we agree and disagree;
this is everyone's experience. But above all,
being fair, sincere, and open-minded to the situation is what matters most.

At any moment, countless thoughts, emotions, and reactions can run through your mind;
if they don't also run from your mouth, you are truly a wise person.

Everyone wants to be a winner; if you are soft-spoken and broad-minded,
that is the truly intelligent path to victory.

CRITICISM AND PRAISE

Don't overly criticize a bad example.
No one knows what might happen later.

Don't overly praise someone just because they show potential.
No one knows exactly what they will become.

Don't pass judgment arbitrarily.
No one knows what the impact will be.

Until you've completed a project, don't proclaim it far and wide.
No one knows what will happen in the future.

Don't indulge your children too much.
That is not the way to help them grow up.

Don't be too full of hate for your enemies.
You might defeat them, but there will still be consequences.

Don't take too much advantage of your loved ones.
Eventually, it will be the source of resentment.

Don't be harsh and critical of those who work for you.
No one will want to be around you.

Don't mistreat your subordinates.
They are likely to hold a grudge.

Don't undermine your friends.
They might grow disenchanted with you.

Don't set a bad example for others.
In the end, it could harm you as well.

You may win an argument through insults,
but it won't truly defeat your opponent.
It is better to stay civil.

Praise and compliments alone don't bring people together.
Cultivate closeness through a loving heart.

Hatred alone cannot defeat your enemies.
Stinginess will not make you rich.

If people excel, don't let your praise give rise to unrealistic expectations.
It's hard to be perfect all the time.

Don't denigrate people who have failed or misbehaved.
It's easy for them to hold a grudge.

Don't celebrate success too early.
It raises hopes that may not be fulfilled.

Don't be overly critical of those who can't find their way in the world.
They might become demoralized.

COMMUNICATION

Don't be overly talkative.
Think about what you want to say and only say as much as you need.

Don't act on whatever crosses your mind.
Whatever action you take, make sure it is productive.

Don't agree to every request.
But if you do agree, be sure to follow through.

If you've dirtied your hands, don't expect social acceptance.
Be a good person.

If you blurt out everything you know, you won't be invited into group decisions.
Don't be a gossipmonger.

Whenever you speak, begin with a smile.
When you conclude, end with a smile.
Speak clearly and get to the heart of the matter.
Talk for the right amount of time, with eloquence.
Even if you're upset, speak gently.
It's better for you and for others.

Even if you're furious at your enemies, you should remain civil and polite.
Someday you may need an alliance with them.

You adore your children; but if they make mistakes,
you must teach them about consequences.
In the end, that's what love really is.

Whatever advantages you have, don't use them selfishly.
Then they'll sustain you well into the future.

To accomplish your goals, consider the needs of everyone.
That's the best way to build a vibrant future.

DEALING WITH PEOPLE

Don't cede power to bad people.
Don't bring fools to a meeting.
Don't weaken the position of your best people.
Don't label a large group as your enemy.

Don't show your wealth to the covetous.
Don't trust those with bad motives.
Don't take advice from people who lack boundaries.
Don't share your innermost feelings with a gossiper.
Don't tease those with a short fuse.

Don't make a rivalry where you can't compete.
Don't compete with the dishonest.
Don't promise what you can't deliver.
Don't attempt projects where you aren't capable.

Don't give advice to those unwilling to hear it.
Don't ask the wrong person for help.

Don't obsess over the wealth you don't have.
Don't be frustrated with others for what they haven't yet learned.
Don't forget the kindness of others, even if they later become adversaries.

Don't show too much affection with your relatives and loved ones.
Don't share too much of your innermost thoughts with your loved ones, either.
Don't show anyone—even your own child—a prohibited source of wealth.

Don't enjoy someone else's suffering.
Suffering can come your way as well.

Don't boast of your own happiness and success to others.
There are many others just as happy and successful as you.

If a person makes a poor decision at a meeting, don't react critically.
You make your own mistakes, too.

Don't keep reminding others how much you've helped them.
Any impact that you made will eventually disappear.

Your reputation depends on the actions you take;
therefore watch your behavior.

Don't be mistaken between a windbag and someone clearheaded.
Don't be mistaken between the honest and the idiotic.
Don't be mistaken between the liar and the clueless.
Don't be confused between the generous and the con artist.

BEING A WISE LEADER

Whether you are perceived as deep depends on how much you say.
If there's no good reason to speak, remain silent.

Whether you are wise or foolish is determined by how well you read others.
Consider this carefully.

How smart you are depends on how self-sufficient you are.
Be self-sufficient.

When you become an important person, that's when you
most need to have humility.
Don't be too proud.

When you compete with others, focus on showing your skills,
not your arrogance or pride.

The higher your reputation, the more you should keep
yourself down to earth.
Be mindful of your actions.

If you have many admirers, show respect to all.
Treat everyone equally.

Even when a meeting is successful, continue to act and make
plans with moderation.
Don't overdo it.

If you become a leader, avoid acting in self-interest.
Consider the needs of everyone.

When you're happy and doing well, remember others.
Keep others in your thoughts.

BEING MINDFUL

If you're not well educated, you won't belong among teachers.
If you don't watch out for negative actions, you're not fit for a spiritual life.
If you're a deep thinker, don't play dumb.
If you're quiet, don't look like a fool.
If you're brave, don't look for a fight.

HEALTHY RELATIONSHIPS

Share delicious food with others.
Keep the most beautiful, priceless possessions.

Don't let any hateful speech out.
Don't let a hateful enemy in.

Don't be too quick to make friends with someone you just met.
Don't trust someone just because they are somewhat familiar to you.

Don't be gleeful as soon as you have something to be happy about.
Don't show fury as soon as you're upset.

Don't sigh and roll your eyes over just any disapproval.
Don't gush over just anything you like.

Don't turn up your nose if the food isn't delicious.
And don't wolf it down just because it is delicious.

WEALTH AND SUCCESS

The affluent should use their wealth wisely.
Don't overindulge yourself once your basic needs are met.

If you have success, make sure you handle happiness properly.
If you are poor and have nothing, make sure that you handle challenges properly.

If you're excellent, you don't need to talk about yourself endlessly.
Everyone already knows you.

If you're mediocre, don't act like you're special.
Others will think you're ridiculous.

Don't show off your wealth.
It only gives others the wrong impression.

If you have power, but you don't know how to apply it, using force will fail.

If you're clever, but you don't use your intelligence, you'll become foolish.

If you're wealthy, but you don't know how to manage your wealth, you'll become poor.

If you show affection, but you don't truly know how to be loving, you'll build resentment.

If you have high status, but you don't know how to live up to your position, you'll become mediocre.

If you're knowledgeable, but you don't know how to apply your knowledge, you'll become idiotic.

If you have good ethics, but you don't know how to live by them, you'll become amoral.

Invite others to eat at your table; it's always appreciated.

Possessions attract enemies; hide your wealth.

Discussions contain wealth; depend on them to succeed.

Conversations carry consequences; pay attention to your words.

People need friends with different abilities, so get to know many different kinds of people.
The divine moves through your speech, so recite prayers and mantras.

It's better to have a consistent enemy than an unpredictable friend.
It's better to work with a good servant than a bad leader.
It's better to hold a lower position among great people than a higher one among those without character.

If you talk too much, you create conflict. Speak concisely.
Hide your wealth from the covetous.

If you make too many promises, you will break them and harm your reputation;
don't overpromise.
If you don't explain your reasons, even your father might misunderstand you;
speak directly and clearly.

If you don't ask, even your son won't take care of what you expect.
Make your requests known.

If you don't study, you will never learn.
Educate yourself.
If you're not giving, even your children won't stay around you.
You must be generous.

SOCIAL INTELLIGENCE

Connections with your loved ones aren't guaranteed.
Don't disappoint those closest to you.
The relationship could end.

Don't keep your enemies close.
They'll walk right over you.

Never look down on anyone.
No one knows who will need who in the future.

When you work for others, fulfill their requests successfully.
Then you'll know how to succeed on your own.

If you avoid lying and cheating, you'll live in harmony with everyone.
If you speak little and you keep your hands clean, everyone will admire you.

If you have good character and put others first, you will get along with everyone.

Thin-skinned people with small minds are easily upset; don't tease them.
Don't make connections with people who flatter with bad intentions.
Don't feel pity for the foolish and the arrogant.

Even if it seems fun in the moment, don't invest your time and energy in people who can't maintain lasting relationships.
Don't trust dark-hearted people, no matter how sweet their words.
Don't trust strangers or those you don't know well.
Don't start an important conversation with someone who isn't relevant to it.

SIX QUALITIES THAT ARE CRITICAL FOR MEN

First, be generous.

Second, be fearless.

Third, have integrity.

Fourth, compete well.

Fifth, be courageous.

Sixth, know your limits.

These six qualities are critical for men.

SIX QUALITIES THAT ARE CRITICAL FOR WOMEN

First, have a good character.

Second, live with decency.

Third, know how to manage finances.

Fourth, know how to take care of others.

Fifth, have self-control.

Sixth, see the best in your loved ones.

These six qualities are critical for women.

MEETINGS

Don't invest great effort in pointless work.
Pay the proper dues that you owe.
Welcome warmhearted friends with a smile and happy expression.

All meetings should have farsighted focus on the best impact for the future.
Don't focus on the smaller, short-term results.
It's more important to analyze and move toward long-term goals.

Reflect now about previous productive and unproductive meetings and their results.
Think now of the future and what outcomes are needed from a meeting.
Let the failures and successes of others' meetings serve as examples for you.

If people aren't involved in the project, or the timing isn't appropriate, don't invite them.
Without these considerations, the meeting will not succeed.

If people dislike meetings, don't invite them.
They'll just disrupt the discussion.
Don't bring a private discussion into public gatherings.
Everyone will hear the details.
Don't have meetings about projects where there's no capacity to get it done.
Any effort will just vanish.

When you meet with a larger group, you gain broader insight.
When you seek advice from experts, you won't have regrets.
Discussions go smoothly with those who are agreeable.
When you ask questions of the experienced, you make better decisions.

If you say what you want from a meeting too early, you limit the discussion.
If you plan a meeting carefully, you'll avoid many pitfalls.
If you don't reach any decisions, you must extend the meeting.
If a meeting doesn't go well, or it goes to extremes, you must improve it.
If you hold a longer meeting, you'll get to the deeper issues.
If you meet on many different subjects, be sure to choose clear priorities.

When you begin a meeting, it's important to start on time.
The subject should be focused, and you should get to the point.
To end the meeting, conclude with decisions and next steps.

Although there are thousands of subjects that can be discussed,
there are only two things that matter to make good decisions:
One is your natural instinctive ability.
The other is good judgment from confident, detailed analysis.
In brief, the most important thing is to take action.

SIX QUALITIES THAT ARE CRITICAL FOR LEADERS

First, speak concisely.
Second, be open-minded.
Third, communicate honestly and fairly.
Fourth, think clearly and carefully.
Fifth, don't be biased.
Sixth, be less selfish.

These six qualities are critical for a leader.

CONCLUSION

Amazing! Truly astonishing!
To have been to so many places, seen so many philosophies
and spiritual traditions!
To have the sharp wisdom to distinguish between flaws and
good qualities!
To have a clear mind to create this writing!
Through the merit of writing this, my mind is like the great
king of elephants:*
Adorned with satisfaction, happiness, and well-being,
holding the sharp sword of wisdom
that overcomes ignorance, foolishness, and lethargy.

This beautiful, transformative, and excellent treatise, written to inspire great accomplishment, was composed by Sakya Pandita.

* This refers to an image in ancient poetry of a great elephant that wears many ornaments and holds a sharp knife to go into battle.

4

ADVICE FOR A SUCCESSFUL AND HAPPY LIFE

*A Conversation Between Brothers**

FROM AN ANONYMOUS SCROLL DISCOVERED IN THE DUNHUANG CAVES

Eighth to Tenth Century C.E.

* The original title in Tibetan is translated as "A Conversation Between Brothers." The addition of "Advice for a Successful and Happy Life" provides the reader with additional context.

A long time ago, in the land of Golden Hats and the Turquoise Valley, lived two very close brothers. They were inseparable and loved each other dearly. One day, the younger brother, who was just eighteen, had to travel far and wide for his work. Before leaving, he turned to his older brother, who was twenty-nine, to ask for essential and practical advice.

YOUNGER BROTHER: Even though I must leave now for distant places, among all our loved ones, you are the closest person to me. There's no one I love more. I admire you deeply, and I will miss you wherever I go. It's hard for me to leave, not knowing when we will meet again or how long we will be apart.

For young people like me, what advice would you give for living well? Please share some of your insights and wisdom. I will never forget your kindness and your love.

OLDER BROTHER: First, I am saddened by this separation from someone I love so much. But second, we must remember that no one can stay together forever, so there is no reason to feel unhappy or to resist this change. If you care about someone, whether that person is near or far, there are benefits in both situations. Even across great distances, our minds can reach each other as if we were meeting face-to-face. Whether we part today or a hundred years from now, in the end there's no real difference.

If you have any questions, ask me without hesitation. With ease and affection, I will share whatever guidance I can remember.

Giving advice to others is easy. Putting it into practice is the hard part. Whatever advice comes to mind, I will offer it to you as a simple guide. If it resonates with you, take it to heart. If anything is unclear or confusing, please ask me to clarify.

These few words of advice will have great meaning in the long run. If someone gives you wealth, it can be used up or lost. The most priceless gift is true and practical advice. If you take it to heart and apply it to your everyday life, there is nothing of greater value.

HAPPINESS

YOUNGER BROTHER: In this human life, what is the highest form of happiness?

OLDER BROTHER: A happy and contented mind is the highest form of happiness. If your mind is not at ease, no matter how good everything else may look on the outside, that's not true happiness.

YOUNGER BROTHER: How can one create a happy mind?

OLDER BROTHER: If you avoid wrongdoing, you will feel at ease whether you are in a high position or a low position. In general, it is essential to respect the rule of law and meet the expectations of society. Whatever you do, strive to do it well and appropriately. If you break the rules, it only helps your enemies, who may then win the favor of those in power. Then everyone will show you their arrogance and contempt, and no argument will help you. How could anyone be happy in such circumstances?

YOUNGER BROTHER: How does one gain happiness?

OLDER BROTHER: If your mind and heart are not busy and preoccupied, that is the greatest happiness.

YOUNGER BROTHER: If you're active in politics and worldly concerns, does that mean you are too preoccupied?

OLDER BROTHER: Politics also takes place within the mind. If your mind is not agitated, politics becomes easy.

HONESTY AND FAIRNESS

YOUNGER BROTHER: What is the source of good character?

OLDER BROTHER: The source of good character is honesty and fairness. Along with these, you should uphold all the other principles I will share with you as well.

YOUNGER BROTHER: What is the definition of honesty and fairness? And how does one practice them properly?

OLDER BROTHER: Rulers must be just, and all laws must be guided by fairness and balance—that is honesty. In some situations, there may be no established law, but there is always truth and falsehood, right and wrong. There is always a way to distinguish between what to do and what not to do. All these aspects of honesty and fairness must be practiced properly.

To put it simply, if you wish to lead others, you must treat everyone as equally as the open sky and be as honest as a scale. Make truth your guiding principle, and treat everyone impartially.

YOUNGER BROTHER: I understand how these actions benefit others. But how do they benefit oneself?

OLDER BROTHER: If you help others, eventually it benefits you as well. If you harm others, eventually it will bring harm back to you. If you aspire to be a leader who is fair to all, is it right to constantly think about how you benefit personally? When you uphold justice, punishing wrongdoing even in your own son, and rewarding good results even when they come from an enemy, people rejoice, and your leadership earns the respect of all.

Younger brother: If a fair system is not established, how can right and wrong be determined?

Older brother: Without a fair legal system, rich con artists are praised as excellent. The honest poor are looked down upon. Thieves and charlatans are well received. Meanwhile, the destitute and impoverished are treated harshly.

Younger brother: If honesty and fairness are so important, how much courage does it take to uphold them?

Older brother: It is better to die young with honesty and integrity than to live a long life by behaving badly and tricking others. One choice may seem easier or more comfortable, but a cold heart rots from within. Don't live like that.

Younger brother: What if you are in trouble, even though you are honest and fair?

Older brother: That situation is very rare, though it's possible that it can happen. In general, if you do wrong, good rarely comes into your life. If you do the right thing, then life goes well for you.

RECEIVING GIFTS

YOUNGER BROTHER: When should a gift not be trusted? And when should you consider food you are offered distasteful?

OLDER BROTHER: Treat wealth that comes from corrupt sources as you would the appearance of a demon. And if you're lured by an invitation to dine, regard it as something repulsive and disgusting.

YOUNGER BROTHER: But people like wealth. People enjoy food. If someone offers you either, why not simply accept it as a gesture of kindness?

OLDER BROTHER: That type of food or wealth is a snare held over your head. It pulls you in the wrong direction. That's not true kindness. You must treat it like an enemy in disguise.

YOUNGER BROTHER: Aside from that, are there any good-hearted reasons that someone might share wealth or food?

OLDER BROTHER: There are two ways a person may offer these things out of a good heart. First, if you're in trouble and someone wants to show you the right path, they may offer you material support. Second, if you are going astray, others may step in to correct you directly and help you with food or gifts as an act of genuine kindness.

WISDOM

Younger brother: How many ways are there to be wise? How many ways are there to behave? And what does it mean to not waste time in conversation?

Older brother: There are two ways to be wise: First, by being insightful. Second, by being balanced. There are also two ways to behave: You can be forthright and fair, or you can be dishonest and crooked. To not waste time in conversation means choosing not to speak unnecessarily.

In general, to be a decent person, avoid these four things:

1. Acting like a know-it-all
2. Adopting a dishonorable mindset
3. Refusing to listen to anyone
4. Speaking about or promising the unrealistic or extreme

DECENCY AND RESPECT

YOUNGER BROTHER: What is human decency? And what is its opposite?

OLDER BROTHER: To have human decency means you are:

- Forthright, fair, and respectful
- Gentle, kind, and thoughtful
- Compassionate and civil
- Patient and determined
- Appreciative of the accomplishments of others

If you have these qualities, even without intelligence or education, everyone will appreciate you and you will do well in life.

The opposite of human decency means you are:

- Dishonest and cruel
- Unreliable and shameless
- Disrespectful and unempathetic
- Malicious
- Overly arrogant and lazy

No one likes people who act this way.

YOUNGER BROTHER: If you show too much respect, isn't that flattery? If you show gentle kindness, isn't that manipulation? And if someone is fierce, could that ever be heroic?

OLDER BROTHER: Whatever you do, it should always be appropriate for the situation. If you express excessive respect, it becomes flattery. If it's appropriate for the situation, it is respect. If it is appropriate for the situation, gentle kindness is not manipulation. If it becomes extreme, it becomes inappropriate and disrespectful.

What is a hero? When your enemy is cruel and fearsome, responding effectively and courageously is heroism. You don't have to be fierce to be a hero. No one becomes a true hero through ferocity alone. That is not heroism. It's villainy.

YOUNGER BROTHER: If you show too much affection toward your wife, won't others criticize you? And if you're rude, won't it hurt your sweetheart's feelings?

OLDER BROTHER: It depends on what kind of affection you show. The best way to show affection is through sincere love. No one can criticize that. You should never abandon affection over concern of others' judgment.

However, if your affection is ostentatious or could be seen as showing off, then you must be mindful. And if you disagree with her or you don't like something she's doing, that doesn't give you the right to treat her badly.

YOUNGER BROTHER: How do you gain respect?

OLDER BROTHER: If you can satisfy and care for your children, parents, and loved ones, you will earn the deepest respect. If your manager or boss is not upset with you, that too is a sign of respect. If you can achieve this, you will find happiness and ease in whatever you do.

YOUNGER BROTHER: How do you gain credibility with others?

OLDER BROTHER: If you don't lie about anything, people will trust you. When others trust you, you have credibility.

WORKING TOGETHER

YOUNGER BROTHER: If you don't know how to accomplish great works, is there any benefit to completing small projects?

Older brother: If you lack wisdom and intelligence, you cannot complete great works. But if you follow the social norms of right and wrong, you show that you are honest and reliable. Even doing that much is worthwhile. Avoid even minor misbehavior and strive to make positive contributions, however small.

Younger brother: Whatever you wish to do, it can't be accomplished without a meeting. What is the best way to hold a meeting?

Older brother: Whenever a meeting is held, be clear about its purpose and keep the discussion focused. If you do this, there will be little need to make changes later. When meeting about any project, keep an open mind and be willing to use your wisdom. Then success will follow naturally. Avoid doubt and hesitation, internal politics, and petty or divisive reactions. Don't make a big deal out of small matters. If you make these mistakes, big projects will not be completed.

When many people come together to talk, trust the person whose points are most supported by facts. If the goal of the meeting is simply to force others to agree with you, there's no purpose in discussing at all. We can never know in advance who will offer the essential insight. If someone is humble or doesn't seem to belong, don't look down on them—just listen to whoever makes the most important point. Even if you have the facts and must refute other positions, do so skillfully and gently.

Elders may speak directly and say whatever they think. You must consider what they have to say.

YOUNGER BROTHER: In whatever you do or say, how do you get straight to the point?

OLDER BROTHER: Some people speak in a chaotic way but grasp the details precisely. Others focus on the trivial and unnecessary and lose sight of what matters most. The main point is to address the central issue and its key aspects. If a person has good experience and knowledge, ask them questions. That is an unmistaken skillful path.

YOUNGER BROTHER: When you work with friends and colleagues, how do you avoid causing friction or offense? How do you achieve goals together skillfully?

OLDER BROTHER: Whatever others say—whether good or bad—don't be disparaging. Don't attack or be overly critical. Maintain a broad and open-minded approach. Even when you must disagree, raise objections, or reject an idea, never do it in a way that embarrasses your colleagues publicly. Discuss your points gently and kindly. Compare the strengths and weaknesses of each plan, and the work will proceed smoothly and comfortably.

YOUNGER BROTHER: How should you work with a greedy person who has the knowledge or expertise you need?

OLDER BROTHER: A person may have knowledge or expertise, but greed is never compatible with wisdom and fairness. It's better not to associate with a greedy person in the first place. This prevents many problems.

If you have no choice, and must work with such a person, deal with them skillfully and gently. Don't allow them to influence you and stand firmly by your principles of fairness and honesty.

YOUNGER BROTHER: If you stand by fairness and honesty and that provokes the greedy person, what should you do next?

OLDER BROTHER: There's no better technique than resolving the conflict peacefully. Don't do or say anything provocative. Even if you are contradicted by manipulative people, that is not a flaw—it is a sign of integrity. Always remember to do what is right. Never rely on others to define your principles.

GIVING ADVICE

Younger brother: What conditions are needed for giving advice?

Older brother: If you know that the person will not be upset or resentful, and that they are willing to change and improve, then you can give advice.

LEADERSHIP AND COMMUNITY

Younger brother: How do you help your loved ones and your community feel happy and fulfilled?

Older brother: Being loyal, sustaining long friendships, and getting along with others brings happiness to your loved ones and joy wherever you go. When you get along with everyone, you bring harmony to all. Conflict brings the greatest heartbreak.

YOUNGER BROTHER: I see it can truly bring happiness if you can achieve this. But what is the exact way to get along with others?

OLDER BROTHER: Leaders must be fair and reasonable. They should focus on the larger outcomes and avoid being disrespectful or abusive. They must act with honesty and integrity toward the people they lead.

Workers and the community should not be duplicitous, but forthright in both public and private. If everyone thinks with a long view, the future will be bright.

Overall, the community must care for and respect its leaders. When there is respect and social order, the result is harmony and goodwill. When everyone gets along, that is happiness. When everyone fights, that is misery. It's the same within a home.

Leaders should not burden the community with unnecessary matters. When they refrain from this, there is little to dislike, and work gets done easily. There are elders and young people, managers and workers, leaders and the public. It's very important for any culture to maintain some form of social order.

Younger brother: How does one lead others properly?

Older brother: Youth, workers, and the community should not be treated carelessly, like rocks and dirt. That is inhuman. You should care about their families and support their livelihood. Reflect on how it would feel if you were in their position. Do they have a well-balanced life? If you support their families and their well-being, it benefits you in the long run. When you act in this way, people will appreciate and respect you. This is how one leads properly.

Younger brother: Workers may perform well or poorly at their jobs. Good performance is rewarded, and there are consequences for poor performance. Is this system important to maintain? If the leader doesn't point out failures, they are unhappy. If they do, the worker is unhappy.

Older brother: The purpose of consequences is to remind everyone that mistakes should not be repeated. The purpose of rewards is to encourage good work and offer an example to follow. If one person does excellent work and receives no recognition, while another does poor work and faces no consequences, that is not compassion—it only causes confusion.

Younger brother: Should you trust those who work for you or not?

Older brother: It depends. If they are trustworthy, you should trust them. If they are not, you should not. In every group, there are both bad and good, junior and senior, poor and rich, foolish and wise. If you understand the short-term and long-term implications of who you're dealing with, everything goes well.

Younger brother: What is the best gift a leader can give you?

Older brother: If a government leader cares about you, the best gift they can give you is political power. If a teacher cares about you, the best gift they can give you is education.

THE LAW

Younger brother: If you are reprimanded by authorities, what should you do?

Older brother: If you have made a mistake, you must acknowledge it. If you haven't done anything wrong, you should calmly and comfortably explain the true circumstances. If you are innocent, but you respond with anger or defensiveness, it will only create more problems. If you are guilty of what you're accused of, admit what you've done, change your ways, and take steps to regain people's trust.

YOUNGER BROTHER: Is there any reason to distinguish between punishments for those breaking the law?

OLDER BROTHER: Yes, there is a reason to distinguish between them. For juveniles who make mistakes, you should not hold a grudge. For older adults who know right from wrong, there must be consequences.

YOUNGER BROTHER: If someone causes you harm, should you seek revenge?

OLDER BROTHER: Legal justice is the best revenge.

FRIENDSHIP

YOUNGER BROTHER: There are some people who others like who I don't care for. And there are some that others dislike who I appreciate. What should I do in those situations?

OLDER BROTHER: You must remain civil to everyone. If you usually have good relationships, but find you don't like someone, don't embarrass them. Be respectful. If you like someone who others dislike, be mindful and appropriate, otherwise it could cause problems.

YOUNGER BROTHER: How does one behave appropriately?

OLDER BROTHER: Be civil and respectful. Don't be harsh or rude. Allow others to be themselves. In general, if someone never helps you, don't be overly affectionate with them. If someone never troubles you, don't be too hard on them. If you dislike someone, there is no need to announce it. If you behave in these ways, then no harm will come to you, and others won't be disappointed or frustrated.

YOUNGER BROTHER: If you are easygoing and open-minded, is there any benefit to caution and hesitation?

OLDER BROTHER: If you don't consider right and wrong, you invite problems into your life. If you don't take precautions with your food, you could be poisoned. If you neglect your wife, she may turn her attention to your friends. If you don't dress properly for the weather, you may get sick.

Younger brother: If you have many close friends, is conflict likely to arise? Is it better to have fewer friends from the beginning?

Older brother: It depends on how you became friends. Friendships with unreasonable and unstable people always end in conflict. No matter how much you feel drawn to such a person, don't befriend them. But if you make friends with honest and reliable people, those relationships will last. It is good to have many of these kinds of friends. You don't need to become fast friends from the beginning. If you build trust slowly, you won't need to distance yourself in the end.

Once you form a good connection, it's important to nurture it. Always be a decent friend. Small problems may arise but be patient. If you're impatient and critical, your friend may respond the same way. If a friend offers advice with good intentions or does something on your behalf, even if you don't fully appreciate it, don't be ungrateful. You should still acknowledge and repay their kindness.

Younger brother: Why should I repay their kindness if it didn't bring me any benefit?

Older brother: In general, if this person likes you and acts with good intentions, it makes them the best kind of person. There's an old saying: "Repay the bad with good; there's no benefit to repaying the good with bad."

When a person does favors for others, they deserve satisfaction and recognition. No one should forget such acts of kindness. If you forget the kindness of others, they feel unappreciated and disappointed because of your indifference. No one will help you again in any heartfelt way.

If someone asks you for a favor that is inappropriate or beyond your capacity, you must tell them honestly from the start. If you accept a request, you must honor it.

EDUCATION AND KNOWLEDGE

Younger brother: How does one become educated and knowledgeable?

Older brother: Simply put, if you never study, you will never learn. All educated people became knowledgeable because they studied and listened to their teachers. Even if an enemy knows something valuable, learn it. Even if you yourself have a shortcoming, correct it.

If someone is sincere and has a good heart, even if they are critical, you should appreciate them. If someone shows bad intentions, even if they seem affectionate, you should avoid them. All wise ones followed this path to become wise.

It's important for parents and grandparents to teach children whatever is helpful and beneficial. Even mediocre students can improve and achieve at the next level. Of course, an intelligent student can accomplish even more. If you have an intelligent child, but you never teach them, they will never learn.

YOUNGER BROTHER: It's said that it is best for one's first teacher to be affectionate and caring, and one's second teacher to have good principles and not be too wealthy. Why is that?

OLDER BROTHER: When you first start studying, an affectionate and caring teacher is very important. Children don't know how to distinguish between right and wrong. They don't understand boundaries. If the teacher doesn't know how to treat them lovingly, it's easy for the children to ignore rules and get into trouble.

What happens in your childhood shapes your character. Love alone is not enough; a teacher must also be capable and knowledgeable. If a teacher is wise and knowledgeable, children will learn from them and absorb their lessons. After their earliest studies, it's good for children to learn from another teacher who has knowledge and strong principles. This helps children become wiser and more ethical. It's better if this teacher is not wealthy so that the children learn the values of simplicity, contentment, and humility. This way the children gain good lessons and real-life experience. They learn how to live simply and face life's challenges.

WEALTH, LEGACY, AND CONTENTMENT

YOUNGER BROTHER: How much wealth does anyone really need?

OLDER BROTHER: Enough to be content.

Younger brother: What is enough to be content?

Older brother: If you have food to eat and clothes to wear, if you don't have to carry water or chop wood, if you don't need to travel by foot, that's enough to be content. If you have these things, you have all you need to be wealthy and happy. If you have more than this, you won't necessarily be happier because you can become a slave to your own wealth. Your wealth can become your enemy.

Younger brother: What you describe as contentment doesn't sound like enough. Isn't it too little if you don't have servants and farmland?

Older brother: Just look at the lower class. They are poorer than you, yet they still manage. What's not enough for you? If you look at the upper class, you'll see endless appetites. A greedy ruler is never content because their ambition knows no limits. They can lose their empire or their life because of it. The clothes you wear and the food you eat should be enough. Especially if you are in a powerful position, you have more and you crave more. The more you yearn for, the more unreasonable you become. You become biased and unfair. All this naturally follows as a result.

YOUNGER BROTHER: If you're poor, how do you leave any legacy?

OLDER BROTHER: The best legacy you can leave is to have lived a wise and honest life. Bravery and skill are the next best. Reliability and integrity also matter greatly. Wealth and prosperity are a lesser type of legacy.

YOUNGER BROTHER: In general, whatever you do, it seems easier to accomplish something if you're wealthy and powerful. If you're poor and powerless, it's hard to accomplish anything. Isn't that true?

OLDER BROTHER: Actually, if you are not honest and fair, it's not easy to accomplish much. Power and authority are closely tied to tragedy. Wealth is closely tied to danger.

If you want greater wealth and power, you must establish a foundation of human decency. What is human decency? It is honesty, fairness, and contentment. Even those who live simply and humbly can embody this, so of course the wise and intelligent can as well.

In general, if you are rich but don't know how to use your wealth, it will ruin you. If you are wise but don't know how to communicate well, it will ruin you. If the rich misuse wealth, it brings tragedy. If the wise misuse speech, it can be hurtful and turn others against them. That is why the wealthy must use their resources properly and positively. That is why the wise must use their speech gently and expertly. When the wise speak eloquently, that's the best communication. If you know how to use your resources properly, that is true wealth.

There's an old saying: "If you speak wisely, your mouth is a gateway to glory. Your tongue is a magic key. If you speak foolishly, your mouth is a gateway to controversy. Your tongue is a demon's axe."

Learn from this example and don't engage in:

- Hurtful speech
- Disparagement of others
- Fighting against authority
- Unnecessary rivalry
- Spying
- Betrayal

In general, if you don't know your own limitations, you cannot understand others. No one knows what the future holds, who will be powerful or weak. You should get along with everyone and don't cause discord with others. Then there is no resentment between anyone.

YOUNGER BROTHER: Is there any other advice you have on how to accomplish goals most effectively?

OLDER BROTHER: If you follow all this guidance unerringly, then you will be able to accomplish whatever truly matters to you. There is so much that can be done in this world; no one can accomplish it all before they die. The bottom line is that whatever you do, you must understand it clearly and without error. Every word I have shared here holds great meaning. Treat each like a wellspring of advice.

YOUNGER BROTHER: I am pleased and grateful. Your great words have given me wisdom that I will hold in the bottom of my heart.

Once this advice was finished, the wise brothers went their own ways.

ACKNOWLEDGMENTS

I would be remiss not to acknowledge the efforts of others in bringing this book to fruition.

First, I give my thanks to Maura Ginty, who provided invaluable assistance in the translation of these four texts. I rejoice in her knowledge of Tibetan.

Heartfelt thanks go to Josh Godine, who labored many hours in recording and transcribing all the teachings that formed the basis of the introduction, and who made many helpful comments on both the introduction and the four texts.

Uvinie Lubecki fulfilled a number of essential tasks, including reading to me and editing a number of dialogues with me to bring into focus my thoughts about why this book is so important for people today.

Karen Meyers helped immensely in developing the vocabulary of The Way of Living teachings for modern audiences.

My thanks to Chuck Goldman for his continuous work in editing and polishing for grammar, structure, intent, and meaning in all my writings.

And finally, to Shambhala's acquisitions editor Jenn Brown for her expert editing and her assistance on the illustrations, and to its president, Nikko Odiseos, my old friend, for shepherding this project so skillfully from inception to culmination.

All of these people have accumulated great merit in this process, as well as my sincere gratitude.

ABOUT THE TRANSLATOR

Orgyen Chowang Rinpoche is a meditation master and teacher known for his clear, passionate, and joyful approach to personal transformation. Based in the San Francisco Bay Area, he teaches locally and travels internationally, speaking to diverse audiences about how to improve their lives and awaken their enlightened potential through meditation.

Rinpoche is the founder and spiritual director of Pristine Mind Foundation. He has taught at institutions such as Harvard and Stanford, at tech companies including Google, and at major conferences such as the American Psychological Association's annual convention. In addition to his teaching, he has translated numerous Tibetan texts into English, including meditation manuals, aspiration prayers, and works on personal development.

Rinpoche grew up in a remote village in eastern Tibet. At the age of fourteen, he began receiving in-depth teachings and personal guidance from the renowned enlightened master Jigme Phuntsok Rinpoche, one of the greatest

Dzogchen masters of the twentieth century. After nine years of intensive study and practice in Vajrayana and Dzogchen at Larung Gar, Jigme Phuntsok Rinpoche's meditation center, Orgyen Chowang Rinpoche was awarded the *khenpo* degree—the highest academic degree in the Buddhist tradition.

His first book, *Our Pristine Mind: A Practical Guide to Unconditional Happiness,* presents the Dzogchen teachings—the most profound teachings within the Vajrayana tradition—in a way that is direct, experiential, and accessible for modern readers. The book has been translated into multiple languages. His most recent publication, *From Foundation to Summit: A Guide to Ngöndro and the Dzogchen Path,* further expands on the stages of Buddhist practice in a clear and practical way.

Rinpoche leads teachings, guided meditations, and retreats both in person and online, and regularly guides student groups on pilgrimages to sacred sites in Bhutan. Known for his heartfelt, accessible teaching style, he makes even the most profound teachings clear and practical. His mission is to help individuals live fully, die fearlessly, and transform every area of their lives.

For more information about Orgyen Chowang Rinpoche's teachings and upcoming events, visit pristinemind.org.